AKNOWLEDGEMENTS

I am indebted to Anna McVittie, Rupert Cooper, Hilary Shekleton, Gail Mooney, John Illman and Lord Brennan of Bibury QC for encouraging me to write this book; to Fernando Sarmiento Morey for his input on one of the stories and to Hugh Thompson and Richard Fitt for helping me correct and improve it. Last, but not least, to my wife Susan and my children Carolina and Eric, for their invaluable aid translating the manuscript and for their infinite patience in supporting me while immersed in this endeavour.

*To Baroness Hening
with great affect and
love Pedro Morillas
oct 2008*

DON FERNANDO

Pedro A. Morillas

Visit us online at www.authorsonline.co.uk

An Authors OnLine Book

ISBN 978-07552-0437-3

Authors OnLine Ltd
19 The Cinques
Gamlingay, Sandy
Bedfordshire SG19 3NU
England

This book is also available in e-book format, details of which are available at www.authorsonline.co.uk

ABOUT THE AUTHOR

Pedro A. Morillas is a Peruvian, self-made, successful entrepreneur. He was decorated with the "Gold Medal for Industrial Merit" by the Peruvian government for his contribution to industry, was director and president of the most important trade entities of Peru and now he heads a global tourist endeavor from his country.

Email: p.morillas@btinternet.com

PART I
BIRTH OF A CIVILIZATION

PROW TO THE SUN

The primitive raft had been floating adrift for many days. The terrified and exhausted young couple aboard, Pau-Llo and Ko-Lla, had gone astray in the immensity of the frightening ocean. They were being carried by the sea current in the opposite direction towards which they were rowing. The inexperienced navigators had lost all control of their precarious craft some time ago; after trying desperately again and again to get back on their course, their energy had expired. Exhausted, they collapsed on top of their raft and fell into a comatose sleep.

Pau-Llo, the male of the two, lost count of how long they had slept. It must have been for a long time, as the sun was now almost at its zenith, timidly making its appearance amid clouds of mist that rose from the heavy fog that surrounded them. The sun kept appearing and disappearing, making the experience even more mysterious and frightening.

Without no point of reference to steer by, they tried again and again to regain command of the raft through rowing, but to no avail. They became ever more exhausted. Their semi-naked, bronzed bodies were soaked with sweat and shone intermittently under the sporadic flashes of the fugacious sun beams as if painted with an iridescent dye.

1

Everything was hazy, interrupted only by these sudden showers of light.

Were they just hallucinating this phantasmagorical show? Were the Gods trying to tell them something? They panicked at this thought. Or were they just solar beams filtering through the fog? These questions crossed Pau-Llo's adolescent mind. Like any seafarer of his time, 8,000 years before Christ, he had never gone through such a terrifying ordeal. His limited experience was restricted to navigating at sea for one or two days at the most, but always close to the dry land, always with the coast in sight.

The mysterious sea for which they had only respect and reverence, terrified them with its vastness: an immense mass of water which millennia later would be known as the Pacific Ocean.

Sometimes, among the clouds, Pau-Llo's feverish mind seemed to discern the creased and venerable face of Tika, his mother, still sad for their sudden disappearance from their ancestral community but, as always, serene and dignified. This produced mixed sentiments in him; a weird phenomenon that gave him courage. It had always been that way, as though the untameable old lady with her brainpower and body language would rumble a war drum for him, encouraging him to continue his course, whatever he was doing – and he was usually doing it well. There had always been a special alchemy between them. Ti-Ka didn't need to open her toothless mouth to communicate with him, as her eyes said it all for her. She seemed to tell him: "You, Pau-Llo, are destined by the Gods to fulfil great responsibilities."

What was this powerful attraction that was carrying them in the direction of the sunrise? Was it a sort of black magic, a curse from the old feared sorcerer of the tribe in retaliation for their escape? Or was it, as it seemed, that the sun now bigger, and brighter, as imposing as ever, was a gigantic magnet which was pulling them towards its core? Whatever it was, it was terrifying.

Due to an ancestral respect for Father Chan, the creator of the Universe, they knew that they should not, by any means, have their backs towards the sun; they had to face it, to greet it and let its divine will carry them along to wherever it desired; and that is precisely what they did. They turned the raft around so that the prow faced the sun, and Pau-Llo, on his knees with his arms raised to the Creator, pleaded:

"Dear father, please have mercy on us, your will be done oh mighty lord, and take us, your insignificant and humble servants, to wherever you want us to go."

Pau-Llo and Ko-Lla could not have known that at that precise moment they were the first human beings to be transported by what would later be known as *El Niño*, the current which would cause so many meteorological disasters and which was now pulling them to the coast.

They bowed deeply and diffidently in the oriental way, probably learned many thousands of years before, from their Asian roots when their people were still nomads - and went into meditation with their eyes closed for a long period of time. When they opened them, everything looked different, brighter and clearer. Although they still couldn't see any land, they somehow felt more secure, and protected by Father Chan.

Sika-Li-Pu, the all-powerful lord of Kiriwac, already had many concubines, more than enough by anyone's account. However, he had fallen madly in love with the gorgeous Ko-Lla, the most beautiful girl born into the tribe for a long time. She was the daughter of Tu-Pa, his best friend and adviser. This was not well received in the tribe, as everybody knew that the girl was in love with Pau-Llo, the younger brother of Sika-Li-Pu, and they thought their ruler should control his lust for the young girl.

Ko-Lla and Pau-Llo had been inseparable since they were children: they had run around as free spirits throughout the woods, beaches and rivers. His mother had tried to remind Sika-Li-Pu of this, and that Pau-Llo was his baby brother, the last of the twelve she had had, and so warranted special consideration. In spite of all this arguments, the mulish chief had decided that "no matter what, she was for me and that was the end of all arguments."

It was under these circumstances that Pau-Llo, knowing how cruel his brother could be when anybody dared challenge his will, planned his escape from the tribe with Ko-Lla. He knew that it had to be as soon as possible, as there was no hope of a solution. In several long meetings that lasted into the early hours, where they drank large quantities of "*chicha*"- a maize drink made from fermented corn - neither Ko-Lla's mother nor Tu-Pa were able to put any sense into the drunkard chief's head and convince him to change his mind.

Sika-li-pu had always been Pau-Llo's idol, but as a result of the unlimited power he had acquired, along with one or two triumphant forages into enemy territory, he had become arrogant and abusive. This was contrary to the spirit of the tribe which was by nature humble and they hoped that, with the passing of time, their ruler would become wise and prudent.

Once the decision to flee was made, they wondered where they could go. To the north? Should they go to the territory of their ferocious enemies, the Chanquis? Or, in the direction of the sunrise, where their no less abhorrent enemies, the Yapas, lived? They believed that their tribe inhabited the end of the world as, over the centuries, they had been cornered by their enemies into the last remaining land on the coast. The only escape, as far as they knew, was to head south, although since childhood they had known that no one had ever ventured there.

So south it was, into the unknown, but they decided to go by sea, to gain precious time and also because then they could stay close to the coast. This would enable them to escape the hunting party that Pau-Llo knew his brother would send out after them to make them pay for challenging their mighty chief. They had already chosen the raft, the best one available, equipped now with essentials for weeks of survival. They had also destroyed the planks that served as rudders on the other rafts, gaining extra time when the chase started, as it would.

When the news spread like straw catching fire that the couple had disappeared, it was about midnight; the mayhem it produced was equal only to that created when the hamlet was under enemy attack. Much of the pandemonium was due to Sika-Li-Pu´s screaming and yelling. Dead drunk, and in a state of semi-hallucination, he was blaspheming and shouting orders at random, added to the animals' screeching and the ear-splitting noises of the confused people tripping over each other in the dark and chaotic night.

Straying off course for days, drifting through unfamiliar waters and not knowing what was happening, the two young lovers wondered where and when this nightmare would end. Again and again this young man came to the shameful conclusion in his primitive brain that it had been the explosive combination of egotism and the abundance of *chicha* consumed by his brother that had pushed them to the brink of their lives.

"It is too premature be called into the reign of father Chan, the kingdom of the dead ones, or to become damned errant expatriates for life," lamented Pau-Llo aloud.

During those prehistoric times the worst punishment that could be inflicted on anyone was to roam pointlessly through life for ever, like those infected with the plague, knowing that no tribe would ever accept them other than as slaves. To suffer until the end of their days, the long agony caused by the solitude produced by the painful separation from their family, their people, customs, environment; by the separation from their sacred mountain and rivers. To be dead while still living, as if the *paca paca,* that evil bird of bad luck, should have crooned twice at them.

"Why, our Lord? Why father *Chan do* you allow this injustice to happen in your kingdom?" agonized the young man.

In a rage of madness, a fuming Sika-Li-Pu had sent Shapra and his brothers to pursue the young runaways. These brothers came from the cruellest and bloodiest family of the tribe; they had enjoyed killing animals, using the most refined ways of torment, since childhood. Shapra knew that sooner or later the couple would have to touch dry land to replenish their supplies. For this reason they followed them close to the shore, permanently lying in wait for their prey, like animals.

Pau-Llo and Kolla watched the new shore line on their left with the utmost apprehension; they could see no major difference to Kiriwac, their beloved territory. The vegetation was of the same medium height, luxurious, with mangroves and tall trees; only the mountains beyond were different. They suffered neither hunger nor thirst as their provisions of dried meat and fruit, together with rain water collected in gourds, were still sufficient.

After some days, they planned to land anywhere that looked like a safe haven and where they would feel more secure. After many attempts, they finally managed to ride a large wave which ran them swiftly into the shore, where they found themselves on a beautiful and solitary beach.

Less than a moon had elapsed since leaving Kiriwac, and Pau-Llo and Ko-Lla now enjoyed some wonderful and fulfilling days on the beach with a euphoric feeling of freedom. Their anguish and sorrow seemed to have left them as nobody had bothered them, not even the animals which approached these two strange creatures apprehensively in order to observe and smell them. They were like nothing they had encountered previously.

One afternoon when Pau-Llo was out hunting and climbing up a hillside, he saw, to his horror and by sheer luck, the unequivocal silhouettes of Shapra and his brothers on the top of a nearby hillside to the north. They were coming after them armed to the teeth. Carefully unloading the game he was carrying over his shoulder, Pau-Llo began to run as fast as his feet would carry him towards the cave where Ko-Lla was calmly sun-drying some food.

By the time that Shapra and his team had closed in on the couple, they were desperately dragging the raft towards the sea to make their escape; the pursuers saw that the waves were impeding the couple's efforts by repeatedly pushing them back towards the beach. In a panic, the two repeated the operation over and over again - until by good fortune, and just as the assailants were approaching, a huge wave crashed onto the beach, and on its return journey towards the sea took hold of the small vessel; they were lifted on the crest of the wave, which carried them onto the surf and out of immediate danger.

Pau-Llo's vessel was a well thought-out raft, made up of bare logs lashed together with a system of rudimentary false keels and primitive oars. The boat was designed to be handled by a minimum of three persons, so the couple were having a hard time controlling it on their own.

At last, with the adrenaline that only comes with sheer panic, Pau-Llo and Ko-Lla managed to pull heavily on the oars with one final thrust; they passed through the strong surf and into the deeper waters where the swell began. With this final, monumental effort, Ko-Lla lost her balance and fell overboard; she just managed to grab one of the oars dangling over the side, and Pau-Llo could pull his terrified partner back on board.

7

Loaded down with their heavy war paraphernalia, the Shapra brothers struggled deeper into the surf after them, until they were up to their chests and could venture no farther. Some threw their javelins and spears at the escaping prey, while others used their bows and arrows which narrowly missed the young couple. They could hear the hiss of the arrows and whistling of the spears as they sped past them; some hit the raft and became embedded in the wood. All the while, the couple frantically rowed their craft while watching the furious reaction of their persecutors who were screaming abominations at them; the raft veered away out of reach and became smaller and smaller as it headed for the horizon.

Their rowing became more rhythmic and peaceful, but the two didn't dare relax until they could no longer see the coastline. They gave thanks to Chan for having sent them a miracle.

The small vessel turned south once more and they soon lost count of how many days they had continued their escape into the unknown. They touched land more than a few times where they spent several days at the most, foraging for food and looking for a suitable place to settle, until finally finding a sheltered stretch of beach. There was a dry area of land where they dug out a cave which they covered with logs and palm leaves. They found the weather to be pleasant and the hunting and fishing plentiful.

Many moons later, when they were organized and feeling more comfortable and had realized that the world was larger than they had imagined, they began to experience a desire to explore and to visit new lands to the south. One fateful afternoon, when returning from one of these exploratory trips, they got caught again by *El Niño*. The raft did not obey their commands; rather than heading back north, where they wanted to go, the sea current was pulling them in the opposite direction.

By early dawn, they had spent the entire night trying to

get back on course. They managed to make a little leeway but at a huge physical cost and they were both on the brink of exhaustion. Only fear kept them awake.

In spite of the fog that hid the stars and all the other celestial bodies, they were sure that they were not just circling around, but rather that the raft was drifting directly into the unknown. They had the sensation of having been swallowed by a huge reptile of gigantic proportion and sliding along its long, wet tongue.

As they advanced the hot weather seemed to change somewhat, moderating a bit, and the fishing was good. At times they didn't even need to use their primitive harpoons or their rudimentary nets, as fish seemed to jump onto the raft of their own free will. After killing them with blows and gutting them with stone knives, they cleaned them with sea water and added *ají*, a variety of chilli pepper, that they had brought along; it seemed to add a magic touch to their meals.

On occasion they were visited by gigantic sea tortoises which, with an excess of familiarity, stayed close to the vessel and accompanied them for days, as did sea lions, dolphins and octopus; some times cormorants, albatross and other sea birds joined them. This showed that dry land couldn't be too far away. Apart from a sporadic, ugly encounter with a stubborn octopus that ended up as food for the couple, they did not confront any serious problems.

One night, they were awoken by a huge jolt and the raft began to shake ferociously. A gigantic white shark had gripped the raft in its jaw and was shaking it from side to side with all the force it could muster. Pau-Llo and Ko-Lla hung on for dear life but everything else on the raft scattered into the blackened waters of the ocean.

Luckily they had grabbed their harpoons at the outset of the attack and they frantically struck at the monster, trying to pierce its thick skin which seemed impenetrable and which rendered the harpoons useless as a weapon. The youngsters were terrified of falling into the water and being crushed, or, worse still, eaten. Suddenly, Pau-Llo lost his balance and went flying over the side into the dark water. "This is it, the end of my life," he thought helplessly.

Only a flash of time seemed to pass between falling, reacting and swimming as fast as he could towards the raft. The shark was almost upon him, jaws opened wide for a vicious attack when Ko-Llo, at her wit's end, used a broken harpoon to land a frantic blow to the shark's nose, stunning it for a few precious seconds. She then dragged her partner onboard and started rowing again frantically. She hadn't thought about what she was doing, but had just reacted spontaneously to the danger.

Although brief, the brutal battle was devastating. The ropes joining the logs had been loosened and frayed, and some of the planks had been lost. To stay afloat, they had to think fast and use their initiative: they braided rudimentary ropes using they own clothes, some fishing nets and bags that hadn't gone overboard.

Naked, with no food and no water, they hadn't the remotest possibility of surviving, only an immense desire that this torment should come to an end and the sooner the better; then father *Chan*, showing mercy, would receive them in the after life. They lay down embracing each other with unfettered passion, in part to protect them from the cold breeze and in part to experience some pleasure as a farewell to this present life. They caressed each other tenderly and under an open sky, with the flickering stars as witnesses, they made love as if it were the last time of their lives, then fell into a deep sleep.

The burning sun awoke them near mid-day. The powerful sun rays had combined dangerously with the marine breeze to blister their dark skin; they found they had bloody, open wounds on their noses and lips, and that their throats were parched which made it hard to swallow and made it almost impossible to talk. Due to the strong sun rays reflecting off the water, their eyes were like two swollen balloons.

They didn't even have the energy to finish off the flying fish that landed on the raft now and then. Days later, when hunger wrenched their guts, Pau-Llo managed, with great difficulty, to bite into the live fish all the while trembling and in great pain as his lips were so badly blistered. He bit some off, and hand fed his partner. They were so confused and terrified at the way the Gods were treating them that they just wanted to die.

Yet another day went by. Only Chan knew how many had passed! "Why did Sika-Li-Pu forget everything, forget that I am his brother, blood of his blood and send those bloody assassins to persecute us?" thought Pau-Llo. "And what did my mother and Tu-Pa do to avoid all this?" He did not reproach them as he knew them well and was sure they had done absolutely everything possible to avoid it. He would never know, however, that they were the first victims in that horrifying night: when Tupa tried to intervene and to stop Shapra, a terrific blow cracked his skull open followed by a piercing scream that slashed the night like a lighting bolt: it was Ti-Ka overcome by a heart attack at witnessing her son ordering the killing of his best friend.

The drama was gradually coming to an end; any time soon father *Chan* would finally welcome them to the eternal life. Pau-Llo was having these thoughts when seagulls, fluttering around the remainder of the sorry raft and picking up leftovers of discarded fish, distracted their painful gaze towards the coastline that had appeared very dimly on the horizon to their left. Fine-tuning their ears, they could hear the distant sound of waves breaking on the shore. Investing their last drop of strength and with the waves help, they ended up on a beautiful beach.

Where were they? Were they alive? Was this father *Chan's* land?

They staggered erratically like drunkards, zigzagging through the wet sand, but could only manage a few steps forward before collapsing. They lay on the edge of the shoreline until the next day dawned.

As the tide began to rise, the young lovers were woken by lapping waves against their lacerated bodies. They slowly crawled higher up the beach and made their way to the vegetation that would provide shelter from the strong rays of the sun and protection during the period of convalescence. They found a nearby stream that provided fresh water, and they fed on molluscs called *muy muys* that became their only food for days. They were too weak to do anything but extract the *Muy muy's* from their shells with their fingernails, clean the meat with seawater and gulp them down.

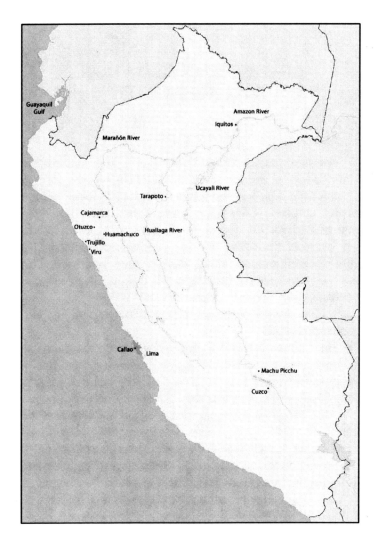

Guayaquil
Gulf

Amazon River

Iquitos

Marañón River

Ucayali River

Tarapoto

Cajamarca

Otuzco

Huamachuco   Huallaga River

Trujillo

Viru

Callao   Lima

Machu Picchu

Cuzco

ADVANCED CIVILISATION:
THE INCA PACHACUTEC: 1460

Weeks had passed since Piminchumo and his brother Cafo, sons of the great Chief Huaman, master of the Chimú kingdom, had left Chan Chan, the colossal capital of that empire.   Chan Chan's population was larger than that of Paris or London at the time, not that either world yet knew of the other, and the Chimú had established a sophisticated culture along the northern coast of what later invaders would call Peru; yet despite its power and prestige, the Chimú were in the process of being assimilated by the powerful Inca civilisation to their south in the mountains

The Chimú princes were travelling into those mountains with more ease now as their coastal physiology had finally became accustomed to the altitude. They yearned for this long journey to end so that they can finally reach the sacred city of Cusco; whose name means 'navel' or 'centre of the earth'. It was a city that irradiated the power and equilibrium that allowed the world, its world, to function.

To maintain unity amongst their diverse peoples and cultures, the Incas were in the habit of taking the conquered princes and nobles with the greatest leadership potential to Cusco for a long season of learning and indoctrination. There they learned the Quechua language, the official tongue of the empire, the art of governing and martial arts. But more than anything else, they learned the Inca philosophy and discipline.

Not that the princes disliked the journey. On the contrary, every day they learned more about the Incas, people who seemed to organise the life of the world with perfection from such a faraway city. They never ceased to admire the discipline of the general and his assistants who had come from Cusco to fetch them, nor the neatness and hospitality in the towns that they visited along the way; parties were organised in honour of the travellers in every important city, with great respect paid for the princes' lineage and ancestry.

The vibrant and devilish rhythm of small drums playing the songs from Cajamarca still pounded in Cafo's ears, the younger, better looking and more laid back of the two brothers. He began to sing and hum the songs, marking the rhythm with his feet. They would love to have stayed longer in the attractive cities that they passed through. But the general had a strict schedule for them.

The young men were amazed by the quality of the Inca roads, as the paths were so well maintained and seemed to be never ending; they were travelling the *capac nan*, the great royal road that ran up the spine of the Inca empire from one end of the Andes to the other. They were also surprised by the system of *tambos*, or resting spots, located in strategic places and distances and used for accommodation and to store provisions for the towns. But what impressed them most was the way in which the general and his companions seemed always aware of what was going on in Cusco as well as in Chan Chan and the great cities that they passed through.

Communication was excellent, sometimes taking place up to three times a day, as *chasquis* or messengers caught up with them from one direction or another, carrying orders, simple goods or news. This formidable system of messenger relay was, along with the system of trails and *tambos*, what kept the empire functioning like a precision instrument. The Inca court was constantly kept up to date about the day-to-day whereabouts and occurrences of their caravan, and Chief Huaman was likewise informed about his sons' voyage and could send and receive news.

Ama sua, ama kella, Ama llulla: "Don't lie, don't steal, don't be lazy," was the greeting the princes learned to hear and give as they travelled along the route.

On the last night before they were due in Cusco, they slept in Huarocondo, or rather tried to sleep as no-one was really able to do so; the Incas because they were now only a step away from their families and the Chimú princes because after such a long journey they were finally going to see the centre of the world. And, above all, to see the most powerful man on earth: the great Inca, the wise Pachacutec.

When they left at dawn Piminchumo hardly noticed as the traffic of *chasquis* and llama caravans started to become more intense along the way. And then suddenly, after rounding a bend, the sacred city lay below them, stretched out in all its grandeur over the floor of an imposing valley. Looking down, he could see fields of crops carved into the sides of the mountains creating a patchwork of different hues under an electric blue sky. Across from them, at almost the same level on the opposite hill, stood the fortress of Sacsayhuaman, jealously protecting the city with its megalithic structure of massive stones. He could see squares and palaces laid out in a trapezoid pattern with geometric precision, and between them streets with people in movement that from this distance all looked measured and purposeful.

"What perfection." exclaimed Piminchumo, the more serious of the two princes and always concerned with his responsibility as heir of his kingdom, "How can my beloved Chan Chan compare to this?"

He was busy with these thoughts when a tap on the shoulder interrupted him. It was the general, who was used to visitors being overwhelmed by these first impressions.

"Piminchumo: the governor of Chinchaysuyo, is waiting for us to arrive before night falls."

On the descent into the valley the people they passed,

many accompanied by llamas laden with cargo, greeted and smiled at them as if they were quite aware who these young men must be. The presence of the general and his people, their attractive clothing and the number of porters, announced to all the winds that the princes were personages of great lineage and authority.

On entering the city, they found themselves walking down narrow streets with imposing walls on either side; the walls were built from gigantic stones, some far taller than a man, that had been fitted together with absolute precision. Before nightfall, after being lodged in a part of the imperial palace, and after bathing and changing clothes, they were then led by the general before the governor of their region.

"Welcome to the centre of the world, noble young Chimús. We hope that your stay with us will be as advantageous and pleasant for you as it is for us."

This was said in Quechua, a language that the young men by now found familiar, although they still did not master it. As if he knew this and to the surprise of the brothers, the noble functionary switched to the Chimú language, which he spoke impeccably:

"In three days we will be received by our master, the great Inca Pachacutec, who will officially welcome you and give you instructions. After tonight's meeting, you will rest for the next two days."

This brief ceremony took place at the door of the governor's sleeping quarters, where the brothers observed the presence of armed guards. In response to the nobleman's signal to follow him, they entered a richly decorated room where a blanket had been spread on the floor. Gold and silver vessels stood on the blanket and two ceramic containers, filled with '*chicha*' reclined against a wall.

The governor and then the general took their seats, inviting the visitors to do the same. Having done this, the princes noticed the presence of two mature and beautiful ladies, who gave the impression of wanting to remain unnoticed; the women remained silent and on their knees, sitting back almost on their heels.

As soon as the princes were seated cross-legged the ladies approached them and began to serve drinks. The general did not speak the Chimú language fluently but the governor continued to speak in this tongue for a long time out of consideration for the visiting princes. He related to them his experiences in those faraway lands and the affection that he held for friends that he had made there. He named places that even they did not know and expressed great respect and admiration for Chief Huaman, their father.

After a while the governor reverted to the Quechua language and told them of experiments the Incas had made trying to acclimatize fruits, flowers and other plants, as well as some coastal animals, to the altitude and vice versa. Just before the time came to leave, Piminchumo took out a bag he had with him:

"My father asked us to give you this small gift, governor, as a sign of his affection"

Taking the fine gold necklace with precious stones in his hand, the functionary thanked them and, smiling, added:

"However, do not forget that when you present yourselves before the Inca, the gifts should always come first."

An equal gift, but of a smaller size, was given to the general. It was only when they stood up to retire for the night that the governor called the ladies over and introduced them as Imac and Shapi. The women did not lift their gaze.

That night, although they were extremely tired, they could not fall asleep; there had been so many new experiences; in the darkness of his room Piminchumo thought to himself: "What a prodigious memory the governor has. He knows so much of what happens and has happened in our lands. But that is why they are who they are: the organisers and governors of the world."

He was deep in these thoughts when a shadow discreetly entered the room. The prevailing darkness made it impossible for him to recognise what or who it was, and an icy coldness momentarily paralysed him. Without knowing what to do, he felt the shadow approaching the place where he was lying. Frozen with fear, he was tempted to call out when the shadow spoke:

"Shh... young Piminchumo, I am Shapi, and I have come to keep you company. Imac is already with your brother."

Calming down and with his heart beating at a normal rhythm again, he took her extended hand and pulled her into the bed. Totally recovered from the shock, he put his arms around her and caressed her, slipping his hand down between her strong thighs, while at the same time searching for her lips with his own. Giving a sigh of pleasure, Piminchumo closed his eyes and smiled. "These people are so organised that no detail escapes them. Is this also part of the learning process?"

Finally, the most important day of their lives arrived: the day they would meet the Inca. Dressed in cream knee-length tunics that matched their sandals, and with multicoloured feathers secured to their foreheads with finely embroidered bands, Piminchumo's red and Cafo's light blue, they wore golden medallions on their pectorals; their arms and calves were adorned with narrow bands of jewellery that had been beaten out for them by some of the Chimú goldsmiths who resided at the palace.

They were escorted by four warriors to the Coricancha Palace, the site where the most important ceremonies of the empire took place. As they cut through a narrow street, the townsfolk stopped to watch the young foreigners walk past.

It was a fresh and sunny morning, with a cold edge to it, typical for the mountains at that time of year. At the palace, guards opened a way for them past gilt walls that led to a large platform area where distinguished looking characters were already seated. The princes were able to distinguish the governor among them; he greeted them with a smile. They came to a stop about ten feet from the platform and soon other young men had reached their places beside them.

Only a few moments must have elapsed, when the existing murmur ceased abruptly, as though cut by a knife, at the sound of a conch: two short low notes followed by a long one, announcing the presence of the Son of the Sun; the living divinity in all his splendour, sitting erect and regal on a litter which advanced borne on the shoulders of his warriors. Military music replaced the notes of the conch and resounded off the walls, creating a solemn and enchanted effect. Beautiful women walked ahead of the sovereign, scattering flower petals in his path.

The entourage approached and the Inca's features were now clearer: he looked about forty-five years old with a strong and formidable bearing. He was a brown figure, not a very good looking man but a muscular one; he looked as if made of solid copper, so dark was his suntan, a consequence of his fondness for outdoor activities, A golden band holding the *llauto* or imperial tassel surrounded his forehead, holding his black shoulder length hair in place and he wore heavy gold and turquoise shell adornments in his ears lobes. His tunic was of the finest woven vicuña cloth and in one hand he carried a heavy gold staff. His distinguished stature exuded the importance of a deity and his grave face dominated the assembly.

When the litter was lowered into the middle of the square, the Inca rose from it and the music automatically came to a halt; everyone fell reverently to their knees. After an instant, the conch re-sounded its solemn notes once more and the court returned to their original positions.

"*Kusicuni chayamuskaykimanta* (Welcome travellers from faraway lands)," announced the Inca in a strong, clear voice. "On behalf of my father, the Sun, and myself, I welcome you and give you our blessings." He continued: "All of the knowledge of our professors and priests is at your disposal. Take advantage of this for your benefit and the benefit of your people. Education is what will make you wise, tolerant and more humble. It is the only path to perfection and towards a better life. Do not waste it: treasure it as the most valuable thing that exists. But at the same time distribute it generously amongst your people. That wealth, like all others, must be shared."

After this short speech the Inca took a seat and his son Tupac, an accomplished soldier, began calling out names and duties. One by one the governors, priests, and professors stood up. He then called the young men by regions. When it came to their turn, Piminchumo and Cafo, now carrying a golden disk, advanced resolutely towards the stage, stopping four feet from the Inca. Depositing their gift at his feet they knelt down before him and transmitted a message of greetings and gratitude from their father. While doing this they looked directly into his eyes. An imperceptible gesture of acceptance and a slight smile was the only thing that they received in exchange.

The Chimú princes conversed with Prince Tupac, an impressive man of athletic physique and feline movements, black mane and a steely look. He would later ascend to the throne upon his father's death with the name 'Tupac Yupanqui', and would take the dominions of the Empire to its maximum limit. Piminchumo got along well with Tupac, a friendship that would last for their lifetimes.

A grand party followed the ceremony, in which the nobility of both sexes conversed with the new visitors, using Quechua as the lingua franca. The Chimús continued to be impressed with the Inca Emperor; when he spoke, it was always directly to the point and with no unnecessary words. Indeed, they couldn't help admiring the whole Inca culture. They were different – and superior - in so many aspects from themselves. And to think that until recently they had been convinced that the Chimú civilisation was the most advanced in the world.

They would never know that other civilisations even

more sophisticated than the Incas' existed in other places of the planet, and that the world was not only what they knew it as, but much more extensive and complex; they would not discover until much later that other communities existed that had not been civilised by the Incas; people who were still nomads, rudimentary hunters and scavengers, living in what would later be called the 'Amazon Jungle', on the other side of the Andes.

THE INCA TRAIL

While the Chimú brothers admired the Incas, the Incas also felt great respect for the Chimú, as they had learned a great deal about certain metal-working techniques from them; they had also copied their sophistication and pomp. It was from the Chimú that the Inca nobility had learnt to travel in golden litters and much of their clothing and adornments were copies of those in the north. The facility with which the Incas acquired knowledge from their subjects, who were often superior to them in some skills, was part of their strength. The sexuality and marked eroticism of the coastal people were also of avid interest to the Andeans, who often acquired concubines from that area.

A year had passed since their arrival in Cusco and the Chimú princes distinguished themselves in some areas and were themselves surpassed in others. They were outstanding in sports such as races and high jump; this was because the diet and permanently benign climate of their homeland that allowed the practice of sports all year round had made them taller. The princes ended up developing their potential to the maximum and became stronger, more mature and wiser than they had been when they first arrived.

It was not difficult for them to make new friends, conquer the female sex, and have 'adventures'. However, they maintained cordial relationships and could be frequently seen with their 'teachers', as they affectionately called Shapi and Imac who were a part of the royal entourage and curiously seemed to feel no jealousy about their love affairs. The princes learnt that it was the custom among the Inca for more experienced older women to initiate younger members of the nobility, a custom they extended to visitors such as themselves.

They found it fascinating to observe the 'kipucamayocs', the official readers of the information contained in the 'kipus': these knotted cords on strings of different thickness, lengths and colours were extraordinary. They were accounting tools that registered the quantities, classes, events and everything that was necessary to record in order to keep the empire able to function.

The time came for the last period of their apprenticeship. The rains had stopped and they prepared for a trip to Machu Picchu, a magical citadel in a heavenly place, where selected young men from all over the empire went to learn the secrets of their professions at the very highest level.

The trip would be relatively short. It would take them three days to arrive and then they would remain there for three months during the dry season, in the wet season the place was almost uninhabitable. The clothes they needed to take were light but included ponchos made from the finest alpaca wool for the cold nights and the altitude. A tutor of the group called Tito was to be the leader and guide of their small expedition.

Early on the morning of departure, after saying farewell to Imac, Cafo met with his brother on the palace's exterior patio and they set off together to meet the rest of the group.

"We will travel on the path that ascends to Sacsayhuaman, and stay there for a while before descending."

These were the orders that Tito gave out as he took the lead. It did not take the well-trained and physically fit young men long to reach the summit of the fortress, as they had made the journey several times during their stay in

Cusco; but, although they had been there on various occasions, the immensity of the rocks and the perfection of their assembly, despite the problems caused by their enormous size, never ceased to surprise them.

After greeting the guards at the entrance, they were allowed to continue up towards the turret, the highest point of the fort. This was a circular construction about five stories high. A stone spiral staircase against the curved wall led them to the highest part of the building; from there, they observed with awe the impressive view over the Imperial City.

"Without a doubt, these are 'mountain people' and they seem to like defying vertigo," pondered Cafo. "Or maybe they want to see how the condor - one of their sacred animals for its strength and power - feels at this altitude." In the opposite direction he observed a large open space where forces of the empire's elite were practising military manoeuvres.

They passed by other temples before beginning the descent towards the Urubamba valley. Later, hiking around the rim of a mountain they observed a majestic valley hundreds of feet below them. Under a clear blue sky, they glimpsed a patchwork of different hues of greens and browns where the farmers had tilled and planted the land. Continuing their descent, the vegetation became semitropical, typical of the deep Andean valleys. Down the steep sides of the mountains were hundreds of Andean terraces consisting of millions of worked stone; and which would have taken hundreds of millions of hours of intensive labour to build.

"How many generations of hard work must this have taken," thought Piminchumo.

It was almost late afternoon when they crossed a hanging bridge suspended above the river. They followed the east bank and gathered a large variety of fruit for their provisions, discovering that the valley was not only an immense garden but an orchard as well. They then walked towards Yucay where they spent the night in a palace belonging to the Inca. The young travellers practiced their dancing with some of the local girls and boys who were watching the dancing steps that were so different from their own with some smiles and curiosity; Cafo, the merriest of the group and an excellent singer, chanted songs from his faraway land in his own language to the admiration of the audience.

Some rain fell during the night and the morning was diaphanous and serene. The sun appeared and its rays were filtered between the tree branches, highlighting the beauty of the flowers and the scenery of this generous land. Tito took the lead again while discussing with Mayta from the Coyasuyo, who insisted - with good reason - that the Colca valley in his homeland was even deeper and more spectacular than this one.

They passed Ollantaytambo, an ancient town with masterful architecture, and headed further along the Urubamba valley towards Patallaqta. Below, the river flowed eastwards in a succession of rapids that changed colour from light brown to muddy white from the foam created as the waters crashed against the boulders in their path. They stopped to admire the majestic snowy peaks to their left; the view was endless.

"The world is so large," thought Piminchumo, "and we are so insignificant."

Was this a premeditated stop by Tito, precisely to foment this type of philosophical thought? It seems so, since neither the leader nor the rest of the group were tired. They all sat comfortably on the top of the mountain and enjoyed the panorama. On the horizon, the sky seemed to unite with the earth in a greyish-blue communion. The group remained religiously silent.

Night was chasing them as they reached their destination, and they were drenched by a rain that refreshed rather than irritated. Now the plants were different and the shrubbery greener, more exuberant and luxurious. The smell of the atmosphere itself had changed; it was the aromatic and sweet smell produced by rain when it hits leaves and combines with the steam liberated from the humid earth.

The next day's stretch was not too long, so they decided to speed up the pace so that they could reach Machu Picchu by nightfall. However, Tito - who knew what he was doing - decided to break the impact of their trip into small doses. They therefore slept in Wiñay Wayna, so as to reach the great citadel early the following morning with the first rays of the sun.

Wiñay Wayna, "Flower of eternal youth", was a small and exquisite inhabited place constructed where the nearly vertical walls of two mountains joined together to form an angle. From afar, the buildings seemed to hang like a balcony from the mountain face, with a mighty waterfall cascading from above, its waters falling precisely in front of the principal construction. The semitropical vegetation and dozens of different types and colours of orchids completed the backdrop to this dreamlike place.

After bathing in the waterfall, they needed to rest in order to reach the citadel the next day at dawn. They planned to wake up before the sun and to jog the last stretch, as the chasqui messengers did.

The day began dark and foggy. The damp path meandered in a pronounced slope around the neck of a steep mountain, as if it were a curved wound etched into the earth by a gigantic dagger. The jog was comfortable and vigorous and the northerners made another discovery:

"Have you realized, Piminchumo, why the steps are so far apart?" asked Cafo.

And before waiting for a reply he answered himself:

"Because they have been constructed for the *chasquis* who jog as we do now, not walk and for the llama caravans that need space to manoeuvre".

The high vegetation formed a roof above the trail

making a kind of humid tunnel, through which the travellers passed.

To their right, the precipice was obviously very deep and they were able to prove this when Tito suddenly stopped, signalling for the rest of the party to do the same: a snake was resting in a coil on the trail. With extreme caution he slid the point of a stick under the reptile and threw it into the precipice. They never heard the sound of the animal hitting the rocks or the foliage. This small incident did nothing to affect their cheerful spirit: it only made them more cautious.

Perhaps because of their impatience or anxiousness to see Machu Picchu, or because of youthful irrationality, the trail seemed long. Finally, they reached the top of another high mountain where suddenly a spectacular view opened up before them.

Unconscious exclamations of awe sprang from them at what seemed to be a floating city. Beautiful light grey constructions contrasted with the surrounding violent greens. Here lay a jewel: a city straddling a mountaintop and wedged between the magnificent surrounding Andean peaks. All this was even more splendid when the rays of the sun, after filtering through the clouds, played over the citadel and revealed tiny houses built on the slopes of the mountain; smoke was spiralling from their hearths.

The young men remained wrapped in silence, not wanting this moment to pass.

As so often in the cloud forest, the clouds were at their eye level; now they rose gently and majestically. At times one could glimpse through the cloud and see that far below, at the base of the mountain, a river, like a fibre of thread, meandered timidly in the middle of a symphony of intense and varied hues of greens.

Green mountains with vertical walls, as if they had been shorn off, surrounded the citadel; they seemed to wrap around the citadel jealously, as if protecting her. Suddenly, everything clouded over again and the young men could not see more than a few steps ahead. They would later discover that because of constant changes in temperature in this part of the cloud forest, the humidity that is accumulated in the vegetation below forms a halo that then condenses into clouds, which ascend slowly due to their lighter weight.

"Nobody can prepare you for your first sight of Machu Picchu. It doesn't matter how skilful the narrator, he will always fall short in his description," commented Cafo, the most enthusiastic of them all.

They noticed some warriors observing them from afar. They also realised that they had arrived at the official gateway into Machu Picchu, "the sun doorway", a small fortification still some distance from the citadel. Moments later they arrived at a second doorway guarded by two sentinels. They approached the high priest who was waiting for them, along with other professors and a group of young women who served drinks and food on a blanket spread out on the floor.

Later, when the Chimús and their friends surveyed the rest of this enchanted place, Cafo exclaimed:

"Nobody can describe this miracle created by nature and man, this sacred communion of the natural, the human and the divine. When I return to my land, it will be very difficult to explain this."

The young men found the altitude lower than in Cusco. The classes, taught by the best teachers from across the Empire, could not have been more interesting; the astronomy lessons held around the *Inti Huatana*, or solar clock, were particularly fascinating.

They practised sports in the main square after classes, where they competed in individual and team events. And when night fell, they were cared for by the ladies who permanently inhabited the citadel.

One of the students' favourite places was called 'Aguas Calientes', 'the hot springs', a captivating spot with thermal waters amidst shrubs of vegetation, hidden at the base of the mountain about a league from the opposite shore of the river. The young men went there as often as time permitted.

When they descended the mountain, accompanied by the resident ladies, it became an unforgettable party. They sang and danced as they descended and the carnival reached its height when they bathed naked in the hot waters.

Emerging from the water, they ran merrily through the vegetation to a shallow stream that flowed placidly nearby, carrying cold waters from faraway snow peaks. Steam was released from their young bodies when they went into the water. They then ran back to the heat of the thermal waters and repeated the process.

"If this is not heaven," commented Cafo, "I am sure that it must be very similar."

And so time passed in this way until one day something terrible happened. In spite of all the recommendations and warnings - especially when it had rained- not to run while descending the nearly vertical slope of Huayna Picchu, the steep peak adjacent to Machu Picchu, a shattering shriek broke the silence of a calm winter afternoon. Somebody had slipped, lost his balance and fallen heavily into the void. It took the body long seconds that seemed eternal to slam against the rocks that lay hundreds of meters below.

"Caaaaafooo!" Piminchumo yelled with all his might, calling to his high-spirited brother whom he did not see amongst those present. When he heard no reply, he ran desperately towards the bottom of the precipice. Moments later, another horrible scream confirmed what they had all feared: it was his brother.

Despite the strong and rooted Chimú belief in life after death, from that moment on nothing was the same for Piminchumo. He frequently isolated himself from the rest of his friends, nor could he stop crying and it was impossible for him to erase the memory of his beloved brother from his mind. He could no longer concentrate on his work, so consequently his return to Cusco was arranged and after bidding farewell to the Inca, his friend Tupac, and the governor, he returned alone to his beloved homeland.

Years later, when the time came for him to become head of his people, he ruled with such dedication, wisdom and affection that he became one of the best, if not the best leader that his people had ever known. He had adopted the Incas' notion that the State has the duty to civilise and to search for the common welfare, a welfare that is created and shared. Ayni, the fundamental principle of the Andean world-vision, the idea that one must share, from the simplest, everyday things to the most significant ones, was for him the only divine moral commandment.

Yet not a single day went by in which he did not remember that moment in which he had lost his brother.

HEADS: I WIN. TAILS YOU LOSE:
AN AWESOME FORTUNE
PLUS AN EMPIRE

Decades later, after the death of the Inca Wayna Capac, Atahuallpa, the son of the Emperor and a Quito princess, came to Cuzco from one of the remote corners of the territory to claim the throne of the empire. Commanding a formidable army he pushed his way recklessly through the sacred Quechua land, and in a bloody battle with the army of his half brother Huascar, defeated them, slaughtering hundreds of thousands of overpowered soldiers. Atahualpa then executed Huascar and assumed the helm of the legendary realm. However, this was to be a Pyrrhic victory.

Months before the Spanish arrived in these lands, rumours spread of white men with beards, riding on top of versatile and unknown animals, carrying with them thunder and lighting in their weapons. It was said that they were advancing in the direction of Cuzco and were approaching Cajamarca, a charming city where the Inca Atahuallpa was relaxing, and where he had the intention of meeting the Europeans in a peaceful way to enquire into their intention; some of his people believed them to be Gods and to have come in a peace.

"Who do they think they are? To claim a realm that is not theirs"

This was screamed by a resentful Asmat, the young and inexperienced chief of the Chinchaysuyo province, the former Moche-Chimú kingdom, and a great-grandson of Piminchumo; he wanted bitterly to avenge Huascar, the former executed Inca, and the death of his own brothers killed at the hands of the Quito invaders. He was an angry man, who resented the presence of the invaders in every key position throughout the empire. For some people he was a shallow and erratic character. Nevertheless, the chiefs attending him paid due consideration to his demands and ideas.

"They have tarnished the honour and dignity of the Inca's institution and have even dared to take some of our concubines with them," alleged an incensed Asmat in one of the secret meetings that were taking place in several locations throughout the empire. These were attended by deposed chieftains of faraway corners of the domain. More than anything else they complained about their lost privileges.

Never before had the Inca Empire been so dramatically divided; never before had it been so large. This handful of dissenters were closing in to make what was to prove the biggest and most irresponsible mistake ever made in Peru.

"We should look for an alliance with the Spaniards, and after a while, when we regain power and composure, we can easily get rid of them. They are just a bunch of individuals, and no match for our mighty army. Or maybe we should make a permanent alliance with them and see how it develops," continued the fantasist Chief. He finished with a harangue:

"My dear brothers, are we going to accept the humiliation of these bastards from Quito for ever? Or, once and for all, make a treaty even with the devil in order to expel them?"

This was a desperate blunder that was going to cost themselves and their people dearly, and which would forever change his world and the future of their descendants.

But the Spaniards, all highly trained and shrewd men,

veterans of a thousand battles against invaders in their own country, had a different stratagem. Knowing well that the empire was in a state of disarray as a consequence of a recent and demoralizing civil war, and that the population was highly disciplined but extremely superstitious, they were planning to take full advantage of these circumstances. They had decided to capture the Inca; once in their power, the rest of his vassals would have no other alternative but to obey them.

By carrying out this ingenious plan, the Spaniards obtained an empire. It was a perfectly played chess game or – as it would be called centuries later - a Machiavellian plot, skilfully engineered: pitting one faction against the other.

As planned, once the mighty Emperor had been taken prisoner in a surprising and well premeditated assault, not one of his soldier dared to raise a finger for fear of putting the life of their divine lord in danger. This explain the question historians have puzzled over ever since: how was it possible that Pizarro, the Spanish conquistador, with a handful of Europeans soldiers was capable to conquer such an immense and powerful empire?

"On behalf of the Holy Roman Catholic Religion and in the name of the King of Spain, I demand you to take our holy gospel and convert to the true religion". These words – an ultimatum - were pronounced by Fray Vicente Valverde, the clergyman who engineered the plan together with the leaders, while presenting the bible to the Inca in the Main Square of Cajamarca. They didn't demand surrender, only his conversion, which did the trick. The Inca, an illiterate person, taking the holy book and observing it with curiosity, lifted it to his ear to listen to see if it would tell him anything. When nothing happened, he impatiently threw it to the ground.

"Oh! My God! The holy gospel is on the ground! Santiago! Santiago! Santiago! - cried Valverde in despair.

What the natives didn't know was that the Spaniards had predetermined a password to attack. This was the name Santiago or Saint James. On seeing their holy icon being desecrated and on the ground, along with the declaration of the priest, the Spanish army sprang into action and massacred the Inca vanguard.

Greed and religious fanaticism were the most important ingredients in the Spanish conquest of America. Another emblematic Catholic figure in the subjugation of Peru was Father Hernando de Luque, a wealthy clergyman based in Panama, who financed the entire enterprise; he was, together with Francisco Pizarro and Diego de Almagro, one of the three partners in this legendary and infamous endeavour.

Once Atahuallpa was a prisoner, he quickly realised that wealth was the most important motivation for the European invaders. With this in mind, he offered to pay a fabulous ransom for his freedom and, in good faith, he made a deal with the Spanish crown. He did this through Pizarro, and the emperor's treasurer present at the moment of the contract: he promised to fill two rooms - similar to the one he was being held prisoner – with gold and four of silver as payment for his release; to which the Spaniards agreed.

Atahuallpa hadn't won wars and taken over an empire as the Inca Emperor only by the brightness of his generals; he was an extremely intelligent young man. A testament to his exceptional qualifications was shown during the months that it took for the ransom to be fulfilled. During this time, observing how the Spaniards amused themselves playing chess, he became interested and after a while and subsequently asking a few questions, he was learned to play and later challenged them equal to equal. History records that he became Pizarro's favourite chess partner.

Meanwhile, riches were pouring in from every corner of the extended realm in the form of incredibly beautiful ornaments. Under cover of darkness, some of the Iberians managed to put aside part of the riches being accumulated. In spite of this, the Inca's order stayed in force until his pledge was fulfilled and the Spaniards had their ransom.

Not withstanding Atahualpa's full completion of his commitment, he was betrayed and executed under the spurious pretext that he had committed fratricide; his troops had executed his half-brother Huascar while at war. In this way, the formal and legally binding contract was never fulfilled by the Spanish Crown. All Atahualpa got for supplying his ransom was his death.

The value of that ransom is beyond imagination: the official documentation lists more than five tons of gold and eleven of silver, so roughly 184,000 ounces of gold and 354,000 ounces of silver. An ounce of gold was then equal to about 10 Pounds Sterling today, and the silver to about 16 ounces per Pound Sterling. By these calculations, the total amount paid on behalf of the Inca was roughly 1,862,000 Pound Sterling. That figure makes the Inca one of the richest men on earth, if not the richest, of his time. If an international tribunal ever decided that Spain had to repay this amount, it would have to compensate the Inca's descendants the fabulous amount of 1,496 billion Pounds Sterling including interest.

PART II

SPAIN, 1591

At the end of the sixteenth century life was hard in Villaviciosa, a fishing village on the Spanish northern coast, in particular for those searching for work. In spite of the discovery of the New World and the great benefits that Spain had thereby received due to this, the wealth, the well-being and culture did not extend beyond the large cities. The exception to the rule was Trujillo, a tiny medieval enclave in Extemadura's sierra, because this town, like no other, had contributed a large percentage of its sons to the conquest of America. For this reason, the town radiated a message of hope for small towns like Villaviciosa and its people.

The message was clear: with no lineage, education or culture, without knowing how to read or write, one could still become rich with audacity and courage. And if luck was on your side, you might even become a knight. Many people had crossed the Atlantic and returned with incredible riches. Many of them had even been given noble titles by the Catholic King and Queen. Had not Pizarro been made a Marquis for his conquest of Peru? And the man was illiterate.

The wealth that the New World had brought so suddenly to the rudimentary Spanish economy had produced, for the first time in history, what centuries later economists would call "inflation", with the sudden increase of acquisitive power in the large cities. The prices of food, goods and everything shot through the roof, putting them further away from the reach of the majority, who, as a consequence, became poorer.

The publican in one of the inns of the little village turned to attend to a patron who was rudely demanding attention at his table, when a figure that nobody had noticed -except for the innkeeper himself – stealthily crept in and grabbed a loaf of bread from one of the tables. He then sneaked out into the street and ran for his life as though the devil himself were after his soul, with his rags flying in the air behind him and the prized bread securely tucked under his arm. The boy narrowly missed the vagabonds lounging on the pavement with the innkeeper in close pursuit behind him, brandishing a huge knife and yelling: "Catch the thief! Catch the thief!" The exhausted inn keeper, after a run for his money, finally caught the culprit with the help of some curious folk who had joined the chase.

The young, dirty, barefooted thief wearing frayed clothes a size too large for him and an old hat that nearly covered his eyes was named Alvaro. He trembled with fear, from the cold and hunger, as he was dragged to the police station amongst the hostile shouts of the crowd that had formed. His thin and pitiful aspect was a familiar figure for the commissary, Sergeant Martin Ruiz de Badajoz y Castilla, as he liked to be called instead of "Sergeant Bacon", the name given him by the town due to his obesity and greasiness.

"Bloody hell. You filthy son of a bitch; when the hell will you learn to respect the law?" he roared in Alvaro's face, poisoning him with his breath, a rank combination of halitosis and the worst imaginable wine. He then added, while bearing his rotten teeth through the thick fuzz of his unshaven face: "This time you're screwed, you hooligan. You've busted my balls and I can't stand it any more.

Dominguez," he yelled, "take this arsehole to the dungeon...and don't give him any food."

Nobody cared, as nobody seemed to care in those times, that the kid was helpless and trapped in the vicious circle of poverty. He didn't have a job because he was not educated, dressed or fed. And he was not educated, dressed or fed because he did not have a job.

Once again, for the umpteenth time, he was back in jail. However, this time he was really in trouble, as ´Sergeant Bacon´ had said: "the dungeon". Damn. This was serious. That was where highly dangerous delinquents ended up. The only escape from here was directly to the gallows or insanity. There was no alternative.

This was an injustice beyond words. There had been no trial or hearing. But, who was there to question the decisions of a drunk, ignorant and abusive commissary? It was true that the boy was a repeat offender or a ´super repeat offender´ as ´Bacon´ affirmed, but his crimes were insignificant. They were all for the theft of food, clothes or other petty things. And who would defend him? The poor boy knew no-one. He had come from Alava with his older brother Rodrigo years earlier, but he had lost trace of him a long time ago as a consequence of one or the other ending up in jail.

"The dungeon" was a dark and dank cave at the end of the jail's interior corridor. It was hardly a yard and a half long by a yard and a half wide, and maybe a bit more in height at its highest point. It had been constructed as a place for torture and hard punishment and thus had no windows, only a door of damp iron bars that covered the cavity leading to the corridor. Due to its narrowness, the prisoner could neither stand nor extend his body completely and the "guests" were not allowed to go to the bathroom. Instead there was a hole in the corner protected by a grille, with a metal trough that discharged into an irrigation ditch running adjacent to the back wall of the prison.

Lying in a foetal position and wrapped in a blanket that stank more than the foul-smelling residues in the trough, Alvaro cried over his bad luck and tried to get used to the fact that he would have to spend days and nights in this deplorable place.

When his eyes had grown accustomed to the darkness, he noticed that he was not alone. An enormous scorpion, imposing and defiant, was roaming inches away from his face with its lethal tail lifted like a mortal question mark. He slowly covered his left hand with the filthy blanket and... Slap. He grabbed it. As the animal fought to unleash its sting, Alvaro used the nails of his uncovered hand to extract its poison, bringing it towards his mouth and chewing it sluggishly. Although its salty flavour was not to his taste, it was something that would entertain his long-suffering guts for a while, at least until he was fed, which he figured would be in two or three days time.

Alvaro noticed that it was night time because of the increasing number of rats that had taken over his cell. The repugnant animals roamed at their leisure over his body covered with the blanket that by now were water resistant due to the build up of filth, and sometimes a daring rat would enter his mouth when he opened it to breathe. He was still not used to the horrid sensation of disgust that he felt when in contact with these animals. However, during the day, while starving and crouching under the blanket, he would avidly watch them, thinking in desperation: "I would love to make a bonfire to roast some of them over a slow fire."

On the third or fourth day his captors finally opened the grill and pushed towards him a bowl containing something like a thick soup. When he tasted it, it seemed the most exquisite dish that he had ever eaten in his life, and this was how his days and nights went by. He no longer cried as he had exhausted all his tears. Outside it was raining heavily. By the Holy Virgin! It was December, when the typical torrential rains of this area did not stop for days. But that year it must have been far worse than before, because the adjacent irrigation ditch was full and its waters were almost overflowing the trough that led into the hole, threatening an invasion of the cell.

It must have been the second week in that hell and there was no sign of any liberation. He felt horribly weak and even his fingernails hurt, as in all this time he had not been able to do any exercise. The poor youth couldn't even stand up straight. Faced with these adverse circumstances, Alvaro was not bitter, because he had never known anything other than misfortune. His will to live continued unabated.

During the desperate night, the water started to seep into his territory so he tried to sleep in a squatting position. He heard a constant scraping sound at the back wall that tormented him and did not allow him to fall asleep. It must have been one or two in the morning when pig grunts accompanied by their characteristic smell suddenly invaded the night. He realised that busy snouts had perforated a hole in the crumbling wall. A ray of moonlight entered the hole and Alvaro, now completely awake, felt around the trough in search of the metal support which he had noticed was hanging from it and was almost detached. He bent it over and over again on the support until it broke; he now had a spatula to help the pigs enlarge the hole.

About an hour and a half later, scaring away the animals, he slipped through the opening with difficulty, sliding and falling onto mud - a mixture of rain, rotten food leftovers and pig faeces. With no strength to get up, he remained on his back on the pigsty floor under the pouring rain. He had no energy to push away the pigs that nuzzled his body and it was easier, much easier and more comfortable to stay in that position. "Fuck it. Let whatever must happen, happen," he thought.

Then suddenly the sole idea of being set free took over and urged him to flee. He straightened up painfully and gained his balance, but was so weak that he kept

41

collapsing; it took all his strength to pull himself up and to stay on his feet. He staggered forward hunched over, shivering under a heavy rain. It was difficult to imagine a more deplorable figure than his. Where was he headed? He didn't have a bloody clue. The only thing that he wanted was to reach the furthest beach from the village and so he set out for the north.

The rain had stopped and the stark light of a sad dawn found him naked, shivering from the cold and bathing in the freezing waters of the sea, near the campsite of a tribe of gypsies. Alvaro was relieved to have washed off the weeks of dirt from his body and to be out in the open air again. An old gypsy approached him and, thinking the young man crazy but moved by his painful appearance, watched him for a long time before throwing him some clothes and leaving. On the second day, after seeing that Alvaro had remained curled up on the ground all day and all night, and thinking him dead, the old man approached him again and verified that he was breathing with difficulty. He returned later with a loaf of bread and some wine, which he placed beside the young man's feet.

The gypsies adopted Alvaro and took him under their wing. After a period of convalescence and being cared for by the tribe, little by little Alvaro regained his strength and became a great help to them. He was now in charge of looking after the mules, vital for a people that seemed to wither and die if they were not in constant movement from one town to another.

These people were seasoned dealers without any scruples. They were capable of selling blankets that were woven nearby as Persian carpets. They bought swords, daggers and old knives, cleaned them carefully, erased their origin of make and coarsely added 'Toledo', in order to increase their value. Sometimes they bought rickety carriages and fixed them in a way that attracted the eye but only lasted a few days, just enough time for them to pull up their stakes and disappear. If the wheels lacked axles and making them out of steel was expensive, then they made them out of wood and lubricated them with some raw meat and *voilà*. After the test period, when it was too late, the buyer discovered from the stench or by the breakage of the piece that he had been tricked.

This was how Alvaro wandered from one town to another, experiencing shortages and cold but having fun and bending over double with laughter. Travelling with the gypsies, he got to know almost all of north-west Spain.

Alvaro loved his new way of life until one day, drunk with love and wine; he had to leave his beloved adoptive family. People said that it was a knife duel with another gypsy for the love of Carmela, a beautiful gypsy girl with a voluptuous walk and large black eyes that only seem to exist in that race. When nerves calmed down and as luckily "the blood did not reach the river", as the gypsies say after a duel, it was Alvaro who had to leave the tribe, as he was the outsider, a *payo*, not a gypsy.

Almost four years had passed since he had been found by these people and Alvaro had grown into a good looking young man. He was about eighteen years old and had worked only for food for nearly two years for Jose Manuel, the old gypsy who saved his life. He thus felt that he had paid his debt of gratitude, with added interest.

Once again he was alone in the world, and as there was no organised mail and he had not returned to his hometown, Villaviciosa, Alvaro had totally lost touch with his brother and the rest of his family. However, he now had a trade. He need not survive solely from taking advantage of people, which he had learned to do well, as he could now also play the guitar and sing. And he did this with the vigour and *alma*, soul, that only the gypsy people can.

Sad and alone, he could not prevent the tears running down his young and handsome face. With his guitar slung over his shoulder and a small sack tied to the end of a stick, he headed by foot to the main square of Salamanca, from where he had been told a stage coach would leave for

Madrid. When he arrived, he found that the next coach's destination was Toledo so rather than wait two or three days for the next one to Madrid he bought a ticket for Toledo, knowing that Madrid was close by.

It was a summer day and he found himself standing on the shore of the Tagus River from where he observed the imposing view of the beautiful medieval city of Toledo on the opposite side of the river; a city that had only just been displaced by Madrid as the most important of the Iberian Peninsula. As the medieval era drew to an end, it was one of the most refined European cities of its time, in which Christians, Jews and Muslims lived in complete harmony. This, of course, meant nothing to Alvaro. To him, illiterate and ignorant like the majority of Spaniards at that time, the most important thing was to find a place to work so that he could eat and have somewhere to sleep.

His few savings allowed him to rent a room for a few coins a week on the Corridor de San Bartolome, near the outside walls of the city. He later found work as a guitarist and singer in one of the nearby taverns.

'The Meson del Gallo' was the name of the inn, not known for its great reputation. Maybe it was precisely for that reason that the clientele enjoyed the music that Alvaro played, as well as eating and drinking. There, one could find almost anyone, from the cart driver with money to throw away, to the Mayor who appeared late into the night with his hat conveniently cocked over his eyes to 'create a shadow over himself' and, so he thought, maintain his anonymity. The great attraction for him was neither the food, nor the drink, nor the atmosphere. It was Maria Jose, a waitress with huge "Moorish" eyes, a waspy waist and a chest and hips that when she danced... when she danced, mamma mia. She made the patrons howl.

Wagging tongues commented that among the fat clientele who installed themselves in the darkest corner, with really large cocked hats and wearing scarves even in summer, were the local priest and his friends, who were known as 'the devotees of the Virgin Pilar". Pilar was another waitress, a good-looking one, with a smile as deep as the cleavage that she generously displayed, and the owner of what were without doubt the finest breasts in Toledo.

Alvaro's music was enjoyed by everyone and the owners, a hard working Gallego couple with great commercial acumen, adored him. During the day he worked as an assistant in the kitchen and at night he used his guitar as a weapon to fight the gods.

Unfortunately, the day that he had to leave Toledo arrived much sooner than Alvaro had planned. His affair with Maria Jose had reached the Mayor's ears and people warned him that the Mayor wanted to disembowel him, as clear as that. Alvaro wasn't about to take his chances with such an influential citizen so he gathered his belongings and fled the city immediately under the cover of darkness. After considering his options, he made the crucial decision to embark on the adventure of his life. His long-cherished dream was to cross the Atlantic and join the conquest of the New World.

In order to do this he had to embark at either Barcelona or Cadiz. For some reason he chose Barcelona. Passing through Madrid in the dead of night, in the hamlet of Carabanchel, bandits attacked the stage coach in which he was travelling and stole all his possessions. Not even the guitar survived; worse still, they took the savings from all his years of work.

Following the course of the Manzanares River, walking in darkness and scaring away the dogs that barked furiously at him, he arrived at the 'Puerta de Toledo' just before dawn. Filthy and freezing again, without a single penny, he waited for the enormous door to be opened so that he could make his miserable entrance into the capital of the Spanish

Empire along with the fruit, vegetable and live animal merchants. But where would he go? And who would employ him without his guitar and in such a sorry state.

He wandered the streets not knowing where he was heading. He had no idea that he was walking towards the Plaza Mayor, under the suspicious glares of the night watchmen on their way home after their night's work, these venerable men who slept during the day and worked throughout the night watching over the neighbourhood. With a pole, a small oil lamp and a handful of enormous keys, they patrolled the streets blowing their whistles so that they wouldn't fall asleep and scare away possible scoundrels.

Alvaro passed the Church of San Pedro the Older, walked slowly down a solitary street and stopped dead in his tracks. There laid out before him was the magnificent Plaza Mayor, the principal square

He was amazed by the vast patio surrounded by tall, imposing and identical buildings, constructed over arcades that ran around the perimeter of the paved plaza. Drunkards, vagabonds, old toothless prostitutes and other specimens of human scum, exited the cavernous corner of the Arco de Cuchilleros, where they had piled into its crevices and stairwells to spend the night and protect themselves from the rain and the cold. The gendarmerie was unable to cope with them anymore, and it was dangerous to approach these narrow rank streets after a certain time. These lowlifes crawled out of their holes in small groups, wearing their ragged clothes covered in grime and their tangled hair peering from below their smelly caps.

Sitting on a step and at a loss of what to do, Alvaro meditated. "Is this my future? Into the mud again? Is my good luck streak over? ... No. No way." he replied to himself. "My clothes are far from being like those peoples' and I am neither lazy nor a drunkard." Tired due to a sleepless night, he anxiously waited for the surrounding pubs and inns to open so that he could try his luck. But no one hired strangers, especially when they were in the state that he was in, and neither did they pay attention to, nor care about, his story of the robbery. It was getting late and he was exhausted and hungry. Drifting along, after a while he reached a small market.

While walking amongst the fruit vendors, he picked up a piece of fruit here and there that had been discarded on the ground, and this was his only food for the rest of the day. But as he ate he noticed other boys do the same and they were observing him inquisitively. Although his aspect was not as miserable as theirs, he was, after all, eating from the garbage the same way they were.

"What is your name stranger? Can we help you?" asked one of the boys who introduced himself as Sancho, but who was better known as 'The Rat'.

Alvaro gave his name and related his story, and surprisingly, this time the audience, consisting of four curious boys, believed him and offered to help.

"The only work that exists here is early in the mornings, and it consists of unloading the carts that come from the countryside. It's too late today but come with us tomorrow we will show you how to earn a few coins."

This was how Alvaro, following his new friends, reached a rickety room in the backyard of an old house, only steps away from the small market. Five more boys of approximately the same age lay on animal skins that had been thrown on the floor. Without undressing, squashed between his new friends and covered with old pieces of blankets, Alvaro spent the first of many more nights to come.

Although it was not yet morning, the insistent pounding of the rain on the tiled rooftop awoke him. More rested now and staring at the ceiling. He wondered if he had made the right decision by leaving Toledo. "To hell with it." he told himself, "if I had not left of my own accord, the Mayor would have done it for me. I had to leave by my own means or I would have left anyway, in a wooden box. The bastard was blind with jealousy and swore that he would get rid of me".

Meanwhile, he became accustomed to his new life and the days, although difficult, were far from boring. In truth, he had a good time with his hooligan friends. Alvaro, as the eldest of the group, more or less became their leader. He bought clothes that were more presentable and he began to look with confidence for the ideal place to start working. He managed to find a job as a waiter in the 'Meson del Gato' where he soon won the trust of the musicians who enliven the frisky nights of the Madrid summer. It wasn't long before the day he had longed for arrived, when he returned to his beloved trade, after giving them a masterly lesson on how to sing and how a guitar should really be played.

Nearly a year elapsed and winter was hovering again. "But who the hell cares about the winter now." thought Alvaro.

He was now doing what he knew best and loved to do. And he had his own guitar plus a few saved pennies.

A NEW WORLD, 1598

In a festive atmosphere such as "El Meson" it was impossible for a young, good looking man not to have affairs with the worldly damsels who worked there. This was Alvaro's case. In fact, he was involved with various girls when he came to the conclusion that if he wanted to reach America he needed to stop. He was becoming complacent in his happy daily routine and he felt he should continue his truncated trip to Barcelona, where he finally arrived in November of 1598, after a delay of nearly three years.

When Alvaro enquired about vessels headed to America, while avoiding the siege of thieves and prostitutes that infested the place, he was directed to the harbour master of the port: this official informed Alvaro that the "Arcangel San Gabriel" would set sail for America in one or two weeks; depending on the arrival of a 'blood consignment', contracted by a Mr. Rodriguez.

Alvaro, by then a lad of about twenty-one or twenty-two years of age, had never known his surname or when or where he had been born. The only thing that he knew was that his mother's name was Soledad. This became a serious inconvenience for his embarkation, as the information was necessary in order to fill out the Ships Log of Passengers and Cargo.

Luckily the Warrant Officer of the ship, Don Ildefonso de Sevilla y Suarez, Esquire, an old sea dog who might lack hair, three fingers on one of his hands and some teeth, but never imagination or resources, took him under his wing. And this was how the young man, from one day to the next, became Mr. Alvaro del Mar; 'del Mar' because from now on he would have emerged from a sea voyage as a new person. His date of birth was roughly calculated and he was now ready to embark on the greatest adventure of his life, having paid part of the fee and committing himself to care for the horses and to sing and play his guitar for the passengers during the entire voyage.

"Damn." he would say years later when referring to the 'blood consignment' that boarded the vessel, "what a consignment of poor devils and hooligans." With the exception of a few decent people, who you could count on one hand, the rest must have come out of a medieval jail. Filthy and smelly, with their hair and beards grown out and matted, they had no manners and spoke terrible Spanish. Beside such rough company it was easier to get used to his own new name, one that sounded so good and instilled so much respect.

That stormy morning, ninety-four souls boarded a ship that in every way looked overloaded. But the fragile brig departed, gliding through the thick drizzle and dense fog of a Mediterranean winter.

Many of the passengers were heading towards the unknown, to become rich or go to their deaths. These thoughts, interrupted by rough orders shouted at the crew, were uppermost in all the passengers' minds as they sat with their backs to the bulkhead of the vessel, holding on to whatever they can. The voyage was meant to last three months until Portobello in New Granada, and then a further four to Callao; they would make a stop in Havana along the way.

People who had never sailed before soon began to feel ill; they became dizzy and vomited uncontrollably. Not since his time in the dungeon cell had Alvaro experienced the unpleasant sensation of having a headache and feeling nauseous whilst having nothing left in his stomach to throw up. He prayed that the vessel would stop rolling and stabilise but to no avail. He went down to the cabin to lie down and hoped that it would be better than being on deck; but on the contrary, it was worse. The strong smell of decomposed fish and vinegar impregnated in the *mamparos,* or wooden divisions, made him even sicker. He was tormented by the creaking of the structures, the swaying of the deck head and the chaotic squeals and howls from terrified animals in the hold. This nightmare convinced him that it was better to be outside than in.

Up on deck, the crew had great fun giving out cruel recipes to cure seasickness. "Biting the rope of the anchor is good", they advised. So Alvaro witnessed some unlucky voyagers on one side, green with sickness and fear, unnecessarily ruining their teeth to the concealed amusement of their tormentors. "You must drink sea water with lime", said one of them, and on the starboard side the other poor devils tried to do just this. "Drinking piss with salt is best" cried another.

"All right, everybody. Who's the son of a bitch who's been having you on?". "That's not the cure", yelled a kitchen aide as he handed them a jug containing a greenish liquid, prepared with God knows what nastiness that made them run desperately to the rail to throw their guts up, before the grotesque cackles of the sailors. The captain had to come down from the bridge, swearing like mad, to restore order.

The second day was the same, although, as one could expect, the number of sick people decreased. It is only on the third day that everyone managed to eat part of what they were served and the situation seemed to stabilise. However, the ship did not steady, the sea was still choppy and the vessel was tossed along with no apparent control, like a nutshell riding the waves in the immensity of the ocean.

Alvaro had been no exception to the rule and had tried just about everything, particularly limes, provided by one of the more respectable looking passengers, but nothing seemed to make him feel any better. He thought that if he vomited any more it would turn him inside out. However, his experience as a kitchen aide convinced him that all this must be normal as he had observed that no food had been prepared for the passengers on the first day and only a small amount on the second.

More than a week of the voyage passed by and the passengers were already getting to know each other; Alvaro passed the time by entertaining them with his guitar. They slowly got used to the rocking of the boat and the pestilence of filthy people packed together in a small space by the time they passed the latitude of Madeira.

Later on, a storm lashed out and took them by surprise. The crew could not lower the sails in time and the brig lurched dangerously to port, then to starboard and continued to roll for what seemed an eternity. Huge waves crashed against the bow, raising the ship into the air, making her pitch to and then drop suddenly, the hurricane force winds making it exceedingly difficult to maintain control of the vessel.

Joao Saldanha, the attractive and experienced young Portuguese pilot, resembled a giant in command of the enormous wheel of the ship amidst a pandemonium of waves, rain and conflicting winds. Protected by a heavy hooded raincoat, he remained standing with his legs spread apart and his hands clutching the wheel. Great waves crashed against the forecastle and as far back as the ship's bridge. Joao's weather-beaten face showed no anxiety or desperation, just sturdiness and sheer determination.

The wind battered his face and the rain poured down onto him while he vigorously maintained the course of the vessel. Only God knows what thoughts crossed the mind of this intrepid navigator who, in spite of his twenty-six years of age, had already made nine journeys to America and six to the China Sea. With half-closed eyes he scrutinised the ocean and energetically turned the rudder in one direction and then another, while the waves rose like monsters on all sides.

Under the captain's command, the crew finished hauling the sails in the middle of the uproar of the storm, the screams and the blasphemies. Two helpers had fallen from the yards; one directly into the water and the other had crashed into the ship's rail before disappearing into the sea. Nobody made the least effort to save them. The ship strained against the storm and creaked all over; it seemed that it would break up or capsize at any minute. The passengers and some of the crew were paralysed with fear, and watched with wide eyes as the pilot somehow managed to keep the vessel afloat.

They could only pray and hope that the pilot made no error or that the storm would not snap the ropes that held the cargo in place. If the pilot did not confront the wave at the precise moment, at the right angle and with the rudder in the correct position, it would be the end for all of them. Likewise if the moorings holding the well-stowed cargo broke, the cargo would slide completely to one side of the hold, causing the vessel to sink.

Everyone's life depended on this one man. It was a titanic fight to the death between an apparently weak human being and the runaway elements. The immense waves followed each other one after another, often from different directions as the storm shifted.

More than two hours elapsed like this, a time that seemed an eternity. Yet Joao was still there: firm, immense like a colossus in the middle of tenacious rain, winds, lightning and thunder. Neither the storm nor he had yielded a millimetre. He hadn't made a single error. Shouting, he let the captain know that he feared for the cargo; he could endure longer, but the moorings could not, and they would yield at any moment. The old captain, like all experienced men of the sea, had not interfered with any of Joao's manoeuvres, knowing full well that under those circumstances what a pilot needed most was concentration.

Now the captain made his way with great difficulty away from the bridge, holding on to the slippery railings in order to keep his balance. He left Joao alone in his solitary duel of honour, one against one.

The captain corralled some seamen and headed with them toward the hold. The terrified passengers hanging desperately to the bulkhead watched as an enormous barrel of olives cut loose fell and began to roll madly from one side to another, crashing against everything it found in its way. It ran towards them and only stopped because of a sudden turn of the ship, balanced itself, changed direction and charged towards other passengers who managed to get out of its way just in time.

"If nobody grabs that bloody barrel, it will tear up the ship or kill someone." yelled the captain.

The barrel, totally out of control, had already destroyed the bottom part of the ladder that led to the deck and had become a dangerous weapon of demolition. It then broke the railing that separated the pigs, rolling over one of them, which now fell, bleeding and squealing, while the rest ran wildly in every direction.

The 'Archangel San Gabriel' carried four horses that were under Alvaro's care. These were extremely valuable animals as they had revolutionised transport and communications in the New World. They travelled like treasure in compartments that were especially made for such a long voyage: these were frames specially designed so that the animals would remain standing during the entire voyage. A wide canvas band attached to the deck head passed under their bellies so that they were well supported and could rest at the same time.

The barrel suddenly gathered speed and crashed into the base of the bridge: it broke apart and pieces of wood, together with olives and their broth shot into the air and mixed with the pig's blood. In the confusion, huge rats ran frightened in every direction and a sailor dragged himself along the ground with a fractured leg.

On deck the situation abated, the rain stopped and the velocity of the wind diminished. Joao, his eyes fixed on the sky and the horizon slowly threw back his drenched hood and lifted his face to observe the heavens. He handed the wheel over to the co-pilot and collapsed onto a bench; he sighed deeply and slowly closed his eyes. He remained breathing deeply for some seconds before slowly getting up and going down to check the results of the struggle.

"Long live Joao." shouted the passengers and the crew as he descended into the bowels of the ship. Some had tears running down their cheeks.

While the crew and the passengers determined who was missing and repaired the damage, the captain, the pilot and another officer met on the bridge of command to evaluate the situation.

"This ship is overloaded. It was extremely difficult to manoeuvre", declared Joao. We urgently need to unload around three hundred stone and totally re-stow the cargo, otherwise we will not be able to survive another storm," he stressed.

"East-south-east to Tenerife," shouted the captain and although they knew that they would deviate by taking this course and would lose some days, Joao and the ship's officers believed it to be the correct decision.

The entry that day in the ship's logbook read: "Extremely difficult day, sudden storm with changing winds up to thirty knots and waves over fifty feet high. Approximate duration: three hours. Two losses in the crew: Juan de Dios Morales and Pedro Diaz Del Olmo; one severely injured: Diego Jose de la Jara. We are heading to Tenerife and will reduce the cargo there."

They sailed to Santa Cruz de Tenerife, across from the African coast, arriving in the morning of December 6th, 1598. After spending five days selling off three hundred stone of flour at a loss, they repaired damages, re-stowed the cargo, restocked the ship and raised the anchor, pointing the bow west-south-west. Luckily, the weather was good and the brig cleaved placidly through the North Atlantic. They encountered various weeks of good sailing and according to the navigation charts, and the captain's calculations, they recovered nearly two days that they had lost to the storm. If they were to continue in this way, they could reach Havana near the pre established date.

Alvaro already knew everyone, was popular and now sang in a duet with Joao, who proved to be a magnificent accompanist. When the pilot sang in Portuguese Alvaro became the backup singer.

The men who looked like ruffians were in fact ex-convicts. One Sancho Rodriguez de la Cotera, a miner who had successfully established himself at the infamous silver 'mountain' of Potosi, had travelled especially to the small town of Beas de Segura, his native town in Spain, to contract a "blood consignment", as they were called, of forty individuals to work as foremen in his mines; Indian slaves would do the actual mining, usually until they dropped dead from exhaustion. 'Don Sancho' was now personally escorting the "blood consignment" back to the New World.

It was well known that Don Sancho had himself been a prisoner in the jail of that town long ago, and that his contract was not with the poor devils he recruited but with the governor of the prison, who was his friend. He offered the prisoners what they wanted the most: freedom, a ticket to America and the opportunity to become rich. They were all happy with the arrangement, even the Mayor of the town, who had named Rodriguez 'Beas de Segura's favourite son', as he had been told that Rodriguez had "voluntarily offered to empty the jail of undesirables, and looked for no compensation". Rodriguez, with the help of his friend the jailer, had simply chosen the youngest and strongest men, not caring if they were cruel or abusive.

While Don Sancho's money had not been able to change his rudimentary manners, he was however an interesting and talkative person. He took it upon himself to try to familiarise the voyagers with the world they were headed for. America was such a place of myth and of fantasy – were not all dreams possible there – that in truth they would have believed anything he told them. The passengers enjoyed his stories of the natives and their customs, and of the incredible landscapes they would see. The ladies, only six in number, kept themselves at a distance, holding on to their husbands' arms and pretending not to laugh at his occasionally crude jokes.

Francisco Bustos, a teacher at a school in Granada, and a middle-aged man of imposing appearance, had been contracted by the governor of Santiago de Cuba to start a school for Spaniards and Creoles. The urgency to begin classes had made it necessary to embark him on this uncomfortable ship instead of a galleon. Another passenger Pedro Hurtado de Mendoza, who was a young man of approximately the same age as Alvaro, who was to disembark before reaching Lima, as he had been invited to stay at the house of some uncles who had settled in the city of Trujillo, on Peru's northern coast, a city that had been named after the Spanish city from which so many of the original *conquistadores* had come.

Alvaro cultivated a friendship with Mr Francisco Bustos for two reasons: because he liked this gentleman's manner and found his conversations interesting, and because he desperately wanted to learn how to read and write. The teacher generously declined Alvaro's offer to pay him for the lessons and began to give them to him for free. Twelve passengers soon joined them and eventually the classes' amounted to about twenty, including some of Sancho's "blood consignment". None of them, however, showed the interest and dedication of the lad from Alava. Soon some of them gave up completely while others stumbled along.

They were helped in these classes by a plentiful supply of books, for part of their cargo was a consignment of pot-boiler romances and the newfangled 'novels' that had started to become so popular in Spain and for which there was apparently an insatiable appetite in the Americas. The adventures of a knight called Sergas de Esplandán were avidly followed as he chased infidels and won over the ladies, while the *Amadis de Gaul* had the advantage, as one wag put it, of being so long that by the time you finished it you could start all over again, as you'd have forgotten the story.

One day, the power of the winds increased and they began to blow violently from the south. The sea became choppy and strong waves beat the ship again and again, inclining the brig heavily to starboard. It remained in this tilting and rolling position all day, all night and a good part of the following day, giving the sensation that instead of advancing, it was retreating. Finally, when everything calmed down, Captain Ildefonso noted in the log: "Pushed by the winds towards the Islands of Bermuda for two days and one night. We must get back on course. Two to three days lost."

AMERICA

At dawn on a clear autumn day, after nearly three months at sea, the lookout up in the crow's nest yelled at the top of his lungs: "Land, land!" They were very near the island of Hispaniola, washed by beautiful crystal clear and calm waters; they could see luxurious vegetation and some scattered huts near the beach. It was a glorious awakening and the natives waved their arms as they approached the ship in their canoes, making gestures that they wanted to trade their wares; but the ship continued its course.

This first contact, although distant, with other people, had raised the ship's morale. A crew member held a kind of Mass to give thanks and afterwards they started a party with the last of the wine and the contagious music played by Alvaro and his friends.

"Fifth of February of 1599. Today we passed near Hispaniola Island without stopping as we still have to recover some lost days. All is going well, the crew's stamina is up and we celebrated with a party", was the captain's entry in the log.

They later passed other enchanting islands - infested with *piratas*, the vicious English pirates, they were told - and they did sight some hostile looking vessels with no Spanish flags, luckily at a distance. Finally the day arrived when they spotted the substantial port of Havana in the distance. Four galleons were docked alongside the wharf and another was sailing out of the harbour.

Even though there were some hours before the vessel could anchor, Mr. Bustos and the other passengers already started to bid emotional farewells to their newly made friends and there were embraces and tears all around. For Alvaro it was a sad parting as a deep friendship had been formed between them; he argued obstinately that the professor should accept his guitar as a symbol of his gratitude. The professor insisted that the satisfaction of having been useful was enough of a gift for him. He handed him his address, they embraced, as is the custom with Latin men, and bade their emotional farewell with moist eyes.

The meagre savings he carried and his guitar were no doubt, the most precious and beloved things to Alvaro. However, something told him that although he had not finished learning, the most important thing that he now had was knowledge. He had the intuition that if he could learn all he can, a new world of possibilities would open up to him. He was so absorbed with his thoughts that he had not realised that the passengers had already disembarked. Now part of the crew was ready to do the same because they would spend the next four days at this port unloading and loading the cargo and doing other jobs.

"Alvaro. Hey. Come young lad, come. You have to come with me, man, 'cause I know some places and some people that you will just love. Come on my friend." It was Joao urging him to come down to the port. He bathed, shaved and changed into clean clothes and voilà, he was ready to see the great city.

At first, standing on firm ground seemed strange to him. The ground suddenly gave the impression of moving and he had some difficulty walking; it took some effort to get used to the new steady surface. Later, as they advanced along the dike he started to forget about the swaying ground and they walked down a narrow street that was bordered by two-storey houses with clothes hanging from their balconies. "Same as the ports in Spain." he thought.

They stopped at a door that had a sign that pompously announced the 'Happiness Inn' 'The best accommodation in town' Alvaro had read it on his first try, with no help, and he felt an immense satisfaction.

Joao entered through the door and climbed the creaking steps that lead to the second floor, following the sounds of Andalusian music and feminine laughter. They approached the bar noting that some patrons were playing *muss* or another similar game, while other men and women were drinking at tables clustered around a violinist. They ordered two glasses of red wine, some tapas to snack on and Joao asked for Taísa. The matron who served them was surprised, looked at them contemptuously from head to toe, recognised the navigator, screamed and exclaimed:

"Damn, Joao. What apparition is this? Dear God. Where have you been, you rogue? They told us that you were dead."

"No woman. Hell no. The fact that I have nearly died many times does not make me dead yet, don't you think?"

"Of course not. Let's see, turn around. Yes, it is true. Man. You still have no wings. Taisa does not work today, she took the day off. But if you like we can send for her and let her know that you are here."

"Yes, go on. And tell her that I am here with a friend, who is a fine guy."

Later, having consumed their fill of wine and singing Sevillian song duets, the stars Taísa and Paloma made their entry. "What a pair of delicious females in their prime. Goodness me." contemplates Alvaro with his eyes springing out of their sockets and almost falling off his chair. The girls were twenty-something years old, dark, a mix of Spanish and native and truly an exotic type of beauty, the likes of which he had never seen.

When the day to set sail arrived, it was almost impossible to tear the boys from Havana. Drunk and lost in love, they threw such a tantrum that they had to be carried back to the vessel on the shoulders of two hefty sailors. Captain Ildefonso owed a considerably large amount of money to the pilot and found himself obliged to blackmail him, threatening not to pay his debt if he did not get back to his job. But even then, two more massive sailors were needed to drag the libertines onto the ship; plus two pails of cold water to wipe the enormous stupid smiles off their faces.

In a few days they reached Portobello and for those who were going to South America it was the end of the voyage on the 'El Arcangel San Gabriel'. Alvaro bid a touching farewell to Ildefonso and the crew, especially to his chum Joao, with whom he agreed to meet up with in Peru - a country about which they had been talking a lot recently - as soon as he ended his contract and collected his money.

From here on, they crossed the unhealthy and heated stretch of firm land on horseback until the city of Panama on the Pacific Ocean, where they would board another ship headed for Callao. The human activity was impressive in this tropical settlement, built in haste and without any planning, and where everything was for sale.

Alvaro, regretting the jaunt in Havana, and disillusioned about not having been able to get to see more of that city aside from the lodging house, ventures out with Pedro Hurtado de Mendoza to get to know Panama. He bought a book about South America -the first book that he has ever bought in his life- and carried it proudly under his arm. The book, that demanded so much of his concentration to understand, helped to familiarise him with his destination and to think a bit less of his friends.

However, Alvaro never made it to Callao. Tired with the ship's numerous stops and weary of so much travelling, he ended his trip in Huanchaco -a small fishing cove- some four leagues away from Trujillo. Pedro had a lot of influence with that decision because he had talked so much and so well about his family that Alvaro decided to stay and meet them.

On March 11th of the last year of the 16th century, Alvaro disembarked in Huanchaco on a splendid summer's day, along with Pedro and other Spaniards who embarked in Panama and had come to establish themselves in these lands. On the same ship he entrusted a letter for Joao, informing him of his decision to stay in the north of Peru.

Trujillo, one of the first Spanish foundations in the New World, was a sunny and pleasant city located in the fertile valley of the Moche River, near the ruins of what was once the capital of the splendid Chimú civilisation: Chan Chan, a gigantic citadel with enormous and endless walls made from adobe brick. The city enjoyed a generous spring-like weather all year round and had a population somewhere under four thousand inhabitants. It was the typical Spanish city of America, with priests, a commissar and mayor bailiff of the Inquisition Court; to ensure their faith.

Thanks to the Hurtado de Mendoza family, rich trustees of extensive land and natives in the valley of the Chicama River, entrusted to them by the royal crown to convert the natives to Christianity, Pedro and Alvaro meet other influential locals. It did not take Alvaro much time to realise that there was no way that he could perform his trade - in a city that was so devout and profoundly conservative- where inns and pubs only existed in the marginal areas. The only fun they had was on weekends, after attending Mass.

Fortunately, for a young man who knew how to read and write there was no problem in finding a job. The Hurtados took him under their wing employing him as an administration assistant for one of their estates.

The months passed and Alvaro, now known as "Don Alvaro", was a prosperous employee, popular among the young ladies for his good looks and likeable personality. But more than anything else, for the remarkable way in which he livened up the parties with his songs and his guitar, quickly becoming the life and soul of every party in town. This, of course, also brought him problems because for some reason or just bad luck, he always ended up involved with women who were either engaged or married.

He happened to be involved in one of these fiascos, and recuperating from gunshot wounds in his leg, a gift from a jealous husband, when Joao Saldanha arrived in Trujillo after more than a year. Alvaro was lucky to have miraculously survived the attack; not even his friendship with the Chief Magistrate would have helped him to get out of the pickle from which he narrowly escaped. This libertine was nearly caught in a bed that did not belong to him and he only just had time to grab his undergarments, flee through the window and then leap from one rooftop to another.

After three consecutive days and nights of celebration, during which Alvaro, still limping, played and danced without respite, he and Joao decided to form a society to supply wine and pisco - the local brandy - to the city and all the surrounding towns of the valley. They opened two shops: one for reception and storage in Huanchaco and another for distribution and sales in Trujillo. Joao settled down at the port and Alvaro in the city.

The business was a success from the beginning and after a few years they became rich, leisurely rich. After a long and adventurous bachelor life, Joao Saldanha, now known as Don Juan Saldaña to the locals, settled down and married Rosita Lagos, a beautiful and intelligent lady, by whom he fathers four children, and Alvaro, a bit later, married Isabel Garcia Pimimchumo, a pretty girl of mixed race who was a descendant of a famous Chimú chief.

The relations between the partners were excellent and extremely prosperous. They were among the few who sent their children to study in the Spanish Mother Land and at the same time they were among the greatest contributors to the construction of the Cathedral. It was a time when the city gradually started to take shape. The Plaza de Armas was by then flanked with magnificent, large mansions built on spacious lots, with huge carved wooden main doors and immense windows with a unique style of iron work. Naturally, the partners acquired their own land and built elegant mansions. The ex-convict of Villaviciosa had gone through an incredible transformation. Absolutely nobody would have recognised him as he was now a learned character with refined manners.

THE CAPTAIN AND THE CONVENT, 1680

Unlike the English who populated the New World by bringing their families with them, Spanish men almost always travelled on their own. So, at the end of the 17th Century there were very few Spanish women living in cities such as Trujillo. One such woman was an attractive thirty-five year old widow, Dona Elena de Hurtado de Mendoza. Her husband, a respected doctor, had left her with a seventeen year old daughter and a considerable fortune. Everyone wondered why, being so lovely, she had never remarried.

Because of her strict religious upbringing and deep belief, Dona Elena dedicated her time to social work connected to the Catholic Church and the education of her daughter, who was a boarding student in a religious school. Elena adored and idolised her child and was preparing her to one day enter into a prestigious marriage with someone from her own social upbringing.

Trujillo society was accustomed to seeing the devout Hurtado de Mendoza women regularly attending Mass at the cathedral. They were much more than just mother and daughter: more confidant and friends. Each day the young lady grew more beautiful, becoming the desire of every young man of her generation in town.

As fate would have it, one day Elena attended a party held in the stately mansion of the Marquis of Herrera and Count of Valdemar, located in the Plaza de Armas. It was one of the few parties she considered attending, due to her pious life. A young, handsome captain serving in the Spanish Merchant Navy approached her, and, the moment their eyes met, they experienced a rising passion over which they had no control and which was to fuse their lives together.

He introduced himself as Don Alonso de Carvajal and told her that he was from New Granada and had arrived in Trujillo that same day. He had been invited to the party by friends as he would be in town for the few days it would take the cargo on his ship to be unloaded. The Trujillanas had never seen the young widow so taken with anyone, or dancing with such abandon and happiness. She seemed like an enchanted princess floating on the arms of her suitor through the majestic salons of the house.

"I have never known such a charming and beautiful woman as you" declared the captain.

"You do me an honour, Sir," smiled Elena.

"How is it that I have never seen you before during my previous visits to Trujillo?"

The lady replied coquettishly, "Valuable jewels don't shine every day, you know".

The couple danced and conversed at length until the early hours of the morning, immersed in each other and oblivious to the rest of the guests. Elena discovered that the captain was single, twenty-eight years old and that, although he seemed to be of pure Iberian blood and his grandfather was indeed Spanish, his grandmother had been *mestiza,* of mixed race. She did not pay much attention to this, because in her own family there was a story of a great grandfather who had likewise married a beautiful lady of mixed race. She also discovered that the captain's regular voyages were between Panama and Valparaiso on the Chilean coast and that he also sailed to Spain and the Philippines.

When the party came to an end, the captain offered Elena his arm and her heart leapt for joy when he offered to escort her home. They strolled arm in arm through the streets enjoying each others company, with Elena's loyal servant, Carmen, following behind them until they reached Elena's residence on the Street of the Mirador of Santa Clara. For once, in spite of her refined education, Elena didn't give a second thought to what her neighbours would think. The chivalrous young captain took her hand gently in his, and, bowing, delicately kissed her hand. Taking his leave he asked her:

"I beg you, Dona Elena, that you allow me the honour of visiting you tomorrow at a time you find convenient".

Once again Elena cared nought for the gossips and replied jokingly:

"If your Excellency considers it convenient, tomorrow you are invited to have lunch in my home".

So the next day at noon a handsome carriage stopped outside the front door of the mansion and a radiant captain descended, anxious to know more of this enchanting woman who had stolen his heart the previous evening. Later, when they had finished their lunch and had moved to an inside patio where they sipped coffee, Don Alonso could no longer contain his desire and declared his profound love for Elena.

In only a few days, Elena's life changed radically and a splendid light had suddenly shone onto the uncertainty of her life. She blossomed from a reserved matron into the happy and uninhibited young woman she had been twenty years before. The sudden rejuvenation was such that Elena now chose to wear bright, happy colours and, later, lower necklines.

Sadly, the inevitable day arrived when the "Santa Eulalia", the captain's ship, had to set sail. And the tearful, disconsolate lady was embraced by her lover who, with tears in his eyes, promised to love her for eternity. He planed to return to Cartagena in New Granada to speak to his family and begin the arrangements necessary to formalise his commitment to Elena, as soon as he had delivered his cargo to Chile.

The weeks passed by slowly and arduously, turning into months that seemed like an eternity, while Elena anxiously awaited the absent lover's passionate love letters and his return. One day, not being able to contain her impatience any longer, and using the pretext of needing fresh air, Elena decided to go to the port of Huanchaco with her maid Carmen. There, they climbed to the highest outlook that dominated the small fishing town, spread their mantas on the sand and sat, looking out at the uninterrupted view of the vast, enigmatic ocean stretching before them.

From this observatory and the help of an old telescope, Elena scanned the horizon for day after day in the hope that, by a miracle of God, the "Santa Eulalia" would sail into view, or any other ship bearing news. Scanning the horizon and visiting her beloved daughter were now the only things that mattered in Elena's life.

Finally, after three long months and only sporadic news, Don Alonso announced his anticipated arrival at Huanchaco. This time, Elena decided that Alonso was to stay at her home. Throwing conventional behaviour and caution to the wind, she cared nothing about what people would say: she felt young and in love with life. The first night they spent together was unforgettable, particularly for her, as she had spent so many years without the passion of a man in her bed. They only slept fleetingly that first magical night, succumbing to each others desires again and again, not being able to absorb enough of each other until they fell asleep in an exhausted, but happy, state.

Time elapsed. Elena's adored daughter Rosita spent her summer holidays with her mother while Alonso was away on one of his trips, so she missed meeting her mother's fiancé before returning to her boarding school. Elena nervously counted the days and hours until his return and once again the sand and the wind were secret witnesses to her desperate love. The mariner, for his part, could not wait to return to Trujillo and used every excuse to do so.

Alone in her room, standing undressed in front of her mirror, Elena contemplated her figure and noticed what she thought were subtle signs of decay. She tormented herself with the idea that maybe her beloved lover, considering the difference in their ages, could be changing his feelings towards her. It was a thought that consumed her and that made the waiting even more difficult.

Their illicit relationship had lasted a little over a year, and, although the preparations for the wedding were going forward, the couple felt obliged to hide their liaisons. With this in mind, the captain had taken rooms in an inn around the corner from Elena's mansion. To facilitate his furtive nightly visits, Elena gave Alonso a key to the front entrance to her house.

At the end of his forth, or fifth visit, the navigator sadly took his leave to continue his voyage to Panama. The inconsolable Elena climbed the hill above the port to her strategic vantage point and disconsolately watched her lover's vessel sail away over the horizon. The forlorn and tormented woman let out a plaintive cry which almost broke Carmen's heart.

A few days later, Rosita arrived back home on another school break; Elena had decided to take advantage of her fiancé's absence to visit the family *hacienda* and review her finances, where she would spend two or three days with a maid and two trusted servants; a carriage was prepared for her and she began the tedious journey, leaving Rosita with Carmen and the rest of her staff to look after the house.

It so happened that Don Alonso's vessel, which was not as watertight as it might be, hardly made it to Paita, not far up the coast from Trujillo, where it had to undergo urgent repairs. As it seemed he would have to stay on dry land for two to three weeks, Alonso decided to board another ship sailing back down the coast and surprise his beloved Elena.

It was almost eight o'clock in the evening when he arrived at his rooms. He washed and lay on his bed thinking about the great surprise he would give Elena. An hour later he was ready for his furtive visit, patting the key he carried in his pocket to make sure he had it; he headed off in the direction of the mansion, full of anticipation

Opening the door quietly, he passed stealthily through the first patio being careful to make no noise. He slowly made his way to his lover's chamber, where he could see a ray of light shining beneath the door. Rosita, who was using her mother's room in her absence, had just taken a bath and stood naked in front of the mirror, singing softly while combing her long dark hair.

Alonso, thinking that it was Elena in the room and wanting his surprise to be special, undressed in the vestibule and, taking advantage of the dim light, tiptoed towards her, wrapped his arms around her and kissed her passionately. He suddenly realized this woman was not his Elena. The girl, frightened and confused, had experienced for the first time in her life the caress of a naked man and the sensual smell of the male body. Nervously, they separated for an instant and Rosita saw a man totally exposed, his male member standing erect and virile. Only seconds of agitated breathing from the two of them passed before their animal instinct took hold of them and they threw themselves at each other with total abandon, embracing passionately; neither one of them thinking of the consequences.

Without exchanging a word, they realized immediately who the other must be. Confused and ashamed, Alonso gathered his clothes, dressed and departed, leaving behind him a very distressed young woman.

Rosita experienced a whirlwind of contradictory emotions. One moment totally desperate and drowning in shame, and the next, a pleasure for the incredible sensation she had felt in his arms pressed against his throbbing, naked body. Realizing the irreparable damage done to her adored mother she contemplated suicide. Unable to sleep she had made her decision by dawn: she would leave this world by joining the cloistered nuns in the Convent of Santa Clara opposite her home, and stay there until the end of her days.

Alonso felt unhinged; he could not comprehend how he had let this happen. He stayed up all night going through a couple of bottles of sherry trying to decide what to do. By sunrise he was so exhausted he fell asleep but he first made the decision to find Elena as soon as possible, wherever she may be, to explain everything to her.

In the morning, looking terrible, her eyes swollen, Rosita sought out Carmen and explained to the horrified woman, between sobs, what had occurred and implored her to accompany her to the convent. There they were received by the Mother Superior who, giving in to Rosita's supplications and thinking it would only be temporary, agreed to accept her into the order.

It was almost noon when Elena, exhausted, returned to Trujillo. Upon entering the house she was confronted by a desperate servant who hastily related the tragedy that had taken place. Elena's visage slowly transformed and she stoically decided to see neither her lover, nor her daughter. Visibly distraught, she took her rosary and her shawl and slowly made her way to the Cathedral, where, on her knees, only God knows what her prayer was.

Calmly, Elena rose from the church floor and climbed the staircase that led to the bell tower. Without a second thought, she stepped off into the void.

The commotion caused by the tragedy in this small city allowed the news to spread like wildfire and it soon reached Alonso who raced frantically to the scene. On finding the love of his life lying there on the ground, lifeless, he let out a terrible scream and lost all reason. From that day onwards he never returned to his homeland but wandered, totally unkempt and dishevelled, through the streets of Trujillo. In time he lost his mind completely and searched for his lost love in vain until the end of his unfortunate life.

THE VICEROY'S VISIT, 1720

Pelayo "Conejo" Del Mar was a lanky, skinny guy with a perpetual and mischievous smile on his suntanned and freckled countenance; sporting two prominent white teeth that made him look like a scrawny rabbit. That was precisely what his nickname meant - *conejo* is Spanish for a rabbit. A rebellious fringe of messy brunette hair permanently shaded his face and covered most of his forehead, while the rest of his unruly mane reached down to his shoulders, his personal trade mark. This vivacious young man of eighteen was an outgoing character, well liked by everyone who knew him in Trujillo.

To this connoisseur of the most remote villages of the Chicama Valley, who from an early age travelled with his string of mules around the area as a roaming merchant, it was an event that happened only once in a lifetime and he had to be there. The most notable members of local government would attend and to have seen a Viceroy, even from afar, would be a subject of conversation for the rest of one's life.

The camps, called *"ramadas"*, for the visiting dignitaries in Paijan as in San Pedro de Lloc, were almost ready, and the authorities of those towns anxiously awaited the regal envoy, who was arriving any day now with his enormous entourage. The official information circulating was that the Archbishop Rubio y Auñon, the twenty-seventh Viceroy of Peru, had already disembarked in Paita and would reach Trujillo around the fourth of January; nobody could determine the exact date.

It was Christmas time, and outside the town of Paijan a group of natives brought in from the mountains were hard at work, much against their will. They were furious because, like any good Christian, they believed Christmas to be an important festivity that should be spent with their families. However, here they were, God knows for how long, forced to work from sun-up to sun-down in hellish heat and sleeping in a humidity and altitude that felt strange to their Andean physiology.

"The bastards call it *'mita'* [an ancient custom of sharing work for the communal benefit] as if we were to gain from our labour, as if things were the same as in Inca times when we really would receive benefits for our hard work. My God, when will this end?" lamented an old man who had already lost a son due to the change of altitude and lack of medical attention.

"Conejo", who had strayed from his usual route that day to observe the progress of the work sat on his horse and from that altitude watched the hectic activity to finish the saloons, dining rooms, bedrooms and farm yards.

"Someone has to tell him", he heard somebody say. "Someone has to make the Viceroy aware of how much we suffer. Damn it. He's a Christian and must be able to understand us."

Sure enough, at that time, contingents of natives were forcibly recruited, especially in the mountains, and brought to predetermined locations on the coast. Here, they set up *'ramadas'* to accommodate and attend the Viceroy and his eighty-strong entourage of family members, helpers, friends and hangers-on who were travelling with him.

Fifty six of these camps were necessary to cover the two hundred and thirty leagues that lay between Paita and Lima. The logistics were overwhelming, involving everyone from the Chief Magistrate to the last native. But of course, the heaviest burden was always for the indigenous population who did the work, supplied the materials and provisions, thus abandoning their families, plots of land and animals for weeks, sometimes months at a time.

It was common for rascals to take advantage of the Viceroys' visits, extorting money from the people in every place that the entourage passed, even though there were strict laws against this. But, as was common practice, no one obeyed them.

"Conejo" Del Mar whistled to encourage his animals and headed towards Trujillo. His extroverted and happy personality endeared him to everyone in that city, from the most aristocratic residents, who knew the history of his family, to the poorest. He was famous for his stories of incredible adventures, exaggerated to amuse his audience.

"One sunny springtime day on one of my routine trips, I was with my mules near the Town of Ascope, and guess what we saw slowly crossing our path?" he used to begin.

"There was a huge monster of a snake, so big and so long that we had to stop to let it pass; but the bloody reptile was taking so long to go by that after a while, tired of waiting, I decided to jump over it with my animals and continue our journey." "Even now," he used to say years later, "it is probably still crossing that bloody path."

"Oh my God, *hombre*! Do you call that abundance?" was another celebrated one, "You have to be kidding. You have to go to Huaranchal, near the Marañón River, and see with your own eyes what abundance means. The guys there have such a profusion of oranges that they don't know what to do with them all. The kids in that town learn how to swim in orange juice."

He was a rarity in such a closed society where titles and coats of arms were so important. His childhood friends were Manrique, the 'redhead', and Diego Morachimo. The first, with reddish hair and green eyes was, like so many other young men of his age, a result of English *pirata* incursions that sometimes the city walls and the brave defence of the sentinels had been unable to contain. The second was the son of the Cacique Don Vicente Morachimo, commissioner of the towns of Chao, Virú, Moche and Chicama. The friendship that existed between them was deep, cultivated in the stables, where they learned how to ride bareback together when very young.

On the way home, "Conejo" Del Mar lined up his mules and took his place at the end of the file from where, when the path was flat and there was not so much dust, he directed his caravan. "Grandfather Simón Del Mar was right, there is much injustice in these lands", pondered the young man. "People say that his protests in Lima were too strong, that he was defending the native population and the separation of religion from politics, and that he would have been pardoned if he had not quarrelled with the "Holy Inquisition." The old man read a lot and he liked to defend his ideas. He gambled and lost not only his life but all of his properties."

Simon Del Mar was a highly educated person and proud of it, a short and slightly built man with a heavy dark beard shading his Moorish-looking face. He was the by-product of the University of Salamanca in Spain, one of the oldest universities in Europe. A prestigious centre where only wealthy and noble Spaniards sent their most selected offspring to be educated by the cream of the intellectual world; but in spite of its strong conservative teaching, teachers couldn't avoid, from time to time, ending up with some strong free thinkers like Simon. In sum, he was a man willing to stand up to anyone and was scared of absolutely nobody.

In the elegant city of Trujillo the population was preparing for the arrival of the Viceroy, and looked forward to the magnificent parties that would be held over various days in the finest residences. It was a different story in the countryside and Pelayo could see that difference and feel the discontent in the surrounding towns he visited. It lingered in the air. People cursed under their breath because they were afraid of repercussions. They complained about the excessive taxes, the forced labour in the textile factories and the mines. They complained about the never ending debts that their landlords had invented, taking advantage of the fact they could neither read nor write.

The young merchant was one of the first to discover that the Viceroy was soon to arrive at San Pedro de Lloc. He had been told by an exhausted horseman who asked for water along the way and who was heading to Trujillo at full speed.

Later, when "Conejo" arrived at the walled city and was about to bed down his horses for the night, he ran into his friend Diego Morachimo who invited him to his house. Once there, he discovered that Diego's father, the *Cacique*, was getting ready to travel to Paijan with an entourage of counsellors and helpers, to try to secure an interview with the Viceroy. When "Conejo" told him that the Viceroy was already in San Pedro, Don Vicente decided to leave that same morning. He did not wish to wait for him in Trujillo as he had no interest in the parties and banquets, where he was probably not going to be invited anyway. He was looking for a serious meeting: he was going to complain to the King's representative, no matter what the consequences were.

At the Chimú noble's request, "Conejo" Del Mar guided his group travelling through the desert and they arrived at around two in the afternoon. The *Cacique* was invited to take a seat where he awaited the regal envoy in a room adorned with flowers and coloured ribbons. Everyone, including "Conejo", was elegantly dressed and anxious to see the highest ranking authority in the huge colonial territory that extended from one end of the South American continent to the other. Around midday, two tired horsemen from the 'advance party' arrived gasping for breath. Their job was to check the final details of the ceremony with the local authorities.

At around three in the afternoon the bugles of a musical band started to play a military march before the assembled townspeople. "Conejo" and his friend were near Don Vicente who was watching the multitude of congregated people, some elegant and others dressed in an outlandish array of costumes. They formed a corridor along which the Viceroy would pass. Finally he appeared, with his stern and flushed face, purple vestments and a black hat with its wide brim falling to one side of his youthful features, giving him the appearance of a spoiled child. He walked quickly, condescendingly stretching out his hand to the notables and looking bored and ill at ease.

The Viceroy was introduced to Don Vicente, who bowed while shaking the extended, limp hand. The noble Chimú respectfully requested a short audience to discuss delicate and urgent matters, assuring him that it would only take a few minutes. Visibly disgusted, the Viceroy responded that he would see him another day with pleasure, maybe in Trujillo, or even better, in Lima. The proud Chimú chieftain politely insisted that it had to be that same day and was rudely shown to a connecting room, where they took a seat on nearby chairs.

From his spot, "Conejo" could only see part of the noble Chimú's face and he could not hear the conversation. He noted the serious expression on the Viceroy's face and his grave gestures, knowing that Don Vicente was complaining about the terrible treatment that the natives were receiving. Barely two or three minutes passed before he saw Don Vicente stand up, bow and bid farewell without a smile.

Cacique Morachimo was angry and did not stay for the official reception that would be held that evening. He rode with his entire party, turning their back on the camp and heading on to Trujillo. "Conejo" was scared; he had never seen Don Vicente so furious. Nobody dared to speak during the entire journey and the only thing that the proud Chimú said was:

"I will have to go to Spain. I will have to see the King."

Don Vicente Morachimo travelled to Spain in 1721 to solicit justice before the King and his Court against the King's representatives and the tyranny they were subjecting the unfortunate natives to. The Chimú was not intimidated, even by the threat from the Viceroy that the privileges noble natives like him enjoyed would be curtailed. Morachimo did not accomplish anything immediately with this journey, but his visit produced a Royal Decree some years later, as a reminder that:

"*The [existing] Royal Decree states that the Indian population is to be admitted to the Church, educated in the schools and promoted to become dignitaries and public officers*". Two instances were cited about recent and illegal non-compliance with this: one on behalf of Don Vicente Morachimo, Commissioner of the Indians and the other by Fray Isidro de Cala, missionary of the province of Peru. The Viceroy and his friends were forced to modify their behaviour towards the Indian population.

However, Viceroy Rubio y Auñon was a weak and lazy character who left most of his official duties in the hands of his undernourished side-kick, a cruel and devilish man better known as "the fat skeleton" due to his advanced anorexia - but ironically, with a huge appetite for gold. Neither of them did anything to improve the situation but exploited the natives in the usual way.

REBELLION AGAINST SPAIN
AND THE MELTING POT

The tremors of the rebellion led by Tupac Amaru, the charismatic heir of the old Inca emperors, were still felt right across the colonial territory, even though he himself had just been hung, drawn and quartered in the main square at Cuzco; but his proclamation of independence and of rights – and respect – for the descendents of the Inca peoples had shaken the backbone of the colonial rulers; they began to see the ghosts of those they had suppressed so brutally so many centuries before now re-emerge everywhere. Even the writings of Garcilaso de la Vega – an Inca prince who had become hispanicised after the Conquest and whose account of it in his *Royal Commentaries* was quite European in outlook - were banned, because they were considered subversive. The authorities argued that it made the natives long for the time of Inca rule:

And there was order and government in which there was an abundance of clothes for the warriors, as well as enough wool to give to the vassals to clothe their families. In the warm climates they gave cotton as payment for the natives to dress themselves and their families. They made sure that the people had everything necessary for human life such as food, clothing, and footwear, that no one would call themselves poor or beg; because they all had enough as though they were rich.

The Royal Commentaries of the Incas, chapter IX.
Inca Garcilaso de la Vega.

One of the first measures taken by the crown as a reprisal for the uprising of Tupac Amaru, was to abolish the privileges of the noble natives for participating or morally supporting the rebellion. Cacique Morachimo, by now old, blind and nearly ninety forced a sad smile at this loss and predicted: "It is the beginning of the end for the Spanish Empire. Tupac Amaru is not the only one who wanted independence; the majority of us want it. They will have to kill us all, and that, damn it, is impossible."

During the last decades of the 18th century the intellectual and political atmosphere was in ferment, not only in Peru but in the entire American continent. The French ideals of liberty, equality and fraternity appealed to the minds of the educated classes, who embraced the ideals of reasoning and free thought.

Such intellectuals began to search each other out to exchange ideas. They put the case for an independent homeland and founded the 'Society of Peruvian Patriots' to promote it; the society published *The Peruvian Mercury*, a periodical with contributors who were not afraid to express their beliefs and criticize Spain's colonial government.

However much the authorities tried to stamp out 'native idolatry' and the revolutionary ideals of Tupac Amaru, there was no putting the genii back in its bottle once escaped, no way of stopping independence – even if it would still take several decades to achieve.

After three centuries of colonial exploitation - made possible by the irresponsible behaviour of a bunch of revengeful natives - the locals finally saw the light at the end of the tunnel in the form of an independent and modern country - or so they thought.

Although independence came inexorably, as predicted, and a Republic was created in 1821, not much changed for the indigenous population, particularly in the vast interior of the country. Some positive changes were made in Lima and in a handful of other cities in the costal area, but the rest was once again neglected. The abuses in some cases were even worse than during the colonial era, and there followed a string of tin-pot tyrannies headed by corrupt and self serving generals who did absolutely nothing to correct the situation.

When Peruvians rid themselves of the colonial yolk, only a handful of Spaniards left to return home, most of whom were royal officers and their families; the rest stayed put. As so often, there was a confusing, fratricidal element to the conflict whereby some members of the same family ended up fighting on different sides and therefore against each other in different armies; some Spaniards fought for Peru, while some Peruvians fought for Spain.

The reason why Peru was the last South American country to become independent was because Lima, Arequipa, Trujillo and a few more cities, were, for centuries, the stronghold of the colonial system in the subcontinent, and it was where the Spanish population was more abundant. These cities, particularly Lima, were home to more noblemen, crown officers and officials than any other cities in South America. They also had the best buildings, opulent palaces and mansions. To give an idea of Lima's importance, it was the first city in America to have a university, the *Universidad Mayor de San Marcos*, and even the first printing press, only recently invented by Guttenberg in Europe.

Peru also had one of the largest populations of "*mestizos*", a mixed breed of Spanish and native people, most of whom were undecided when it came to wanting independence or not; the rest of the population were natives, the majority ignorant and submissive as a result of centuries of exploitation and discrimination. For these reasons, the coalition of the liberated South American countries found it necessary to get together and help Peru achieve its freedom.

What a complicated life Soledad Bracamonte had! This was mostly due to her beauty, and to being the daughter of another beauty, Peta; but her mother had not encountered the same problems as Soledad. Her mother only knew one husband throughout her life: a spouse, who, like a rabbit, had impregnated her with twelve children, given her some basic satisfactions, but no money whatsoever. They were probably one of the very few Bracamonteses living in poverty in that community of large haciendas and rich landlords dispersed among the valleys surrounding Otuzco. Peta's husband had died quite early in life while he was still in his mid fifties.

By 1831, a decade after independence, Soledad was eighteen, but she already had a newborn daughter named Elisa, the unrecognized product of a short-lived romance she had with Valentín, the student son of the mighty Landlord of Chuquibamba: Don Justiniano Herrera, or Don Justi, as everybody addressed the wealthy and abusive leader of the tiny but proud community of Otuzco.

Otuzco was a small town consisting of no more than ninety families, mostly of pure Spanish blood - the majority of them coming from strong Basque roots – and was nestled in the western mountains of the Andean Cordillera at a two-day horseback journey east of Trujillo. It was a rebellious little town, well-known for being an intractable focus of the resistance against independence; it was the last bastion of the recalcitrant royalists still faithful to the Spanish Crown.

Soledad was the victim of relentless harassment by Don Justi, who always managed to force himself on her, despite the courageous resistance she put up against his advances and in spite of the fact that he was also her mother's lover, and the grandfather of her little daughter. But not even this stopped Don Justi's filthy desires and Soledad had no other choice but to surrender to the sexual urgencies of the obnoxious Landlord; she and her family were completely dependent on him.

Don Justiniano Herrera, 'Don Justi', was an

unattractive, smelly, untidy and stout man in his late fifties, always sporting a greasy face and a four to five day unshaved bushy beard; but he was the all-powerful landowner of Chuquibamba, a large estate situated in the mountains along the upper part of the western Andean Cordillera. Don Justi was a rich feudal "gallows and knife" landlord, as people used to call those who personified the law and administered justice to their own convenience in their huge territories, regardless of who was the victim or who was the aggressor.

However, if that was true in the countryside, what can be said of the real authorities in charge of administering justice or applying the rule of law? One President of the Republic used to say, half sarcastically and half seriously: "For our friends, everything. For our enemies, the law." This monstrous misinterpretation created a different golden legal rule to prevail: "Whoever has the gold has the law at his favour." Everywhere in the country, whoever had some power had the licence to apply it as they wished; the exception, of course, being the native population, as they never had any power.

The man was a real stud, as it was well known in the whole region that he had fathered at least fifty children; easily spotted throughout his vast territory by their similarity to their father. Five of them were conceived with his wife Dona Benita and the rest, God knows with how many different, and, for the most part, abused mothers. Rather than feeling ashamed, the man actually boasted about it.

"Hey Justi! Is it true that you have as many as fifty children on your personal account?" was a typical question placed by one of his drinking buddies when they wanted to pull his leg.

"I do not know exactly, but in the last rodeo I held, we counted around that figure", was his normal reply, while sticking out his chest with pride.

The strong evidence of Justi's "brand" was not difficult to spot among his children: clearer eyes and lighter skin, and if they were male, a beard when puberty arrived as the indigenous population did not have much facial hair. It was strange however, to say the least that Dona Benita, his pious and abnegated wife of many years, pretended to know nothing. Nobody knew why - maybe for her strong religious beliefs or for fear of God knows what.

Valentin, one of his sons by Dona Benita, did not have the slightest remorse in abandoning Soledad and little Elisa without any economic help or official recognition. The only imperceptible sign of disturbance on his part was the fact that he didn't come to the estate to spend his school vacations, as he always used to do, since Soledad became pregnant.

As the fame of Soledad's beauty had spread across the region, in addition to becoming Justi's new concubine, the poor young girl had to cope with more unwanted attention. This time it came in the form of a perverted parish priest, "El Cojo" Esquerre, the nickname of the Reverend Juan Esquerre of "La Margarita" parish. He would use all kinds of excuses to come to Chuquibamba to enrol her in a string of religious duties, just to have her closer and in reach of his lascivious hands.

"What could I have done to the "patroncito" to hang me like this for two hours?" lamented the poor husband of Julia, hanging upside down from his feet, his head hovering above ground like the clapper of a grandfather clock. The "Patroncito", or little master, was nobody less than the plump Don Justi, who, feeling horny and wanting to have sex with Julia, another of his victims, had invented offences supposedly committed by her husband to keep him out of circulation for a while. So, there he was, hanging by his feet at the crossbar, allowing the son of a bitch enough time to take advantage of the victim's wife.

As consolation for her suffering, Soledad was now in

love with Alberto Yupanqui, a poor veterinarian who had arrived a few months earlier from the south to work in Chuquibamba; she had found, to her surprise, that he dearly reciprocated her love. With this knowledge, she managed to keep "El Cojo" at a distance, threatening to denounce him and disclose his intentions to the public; but she still had no solution to the attacks of her powerful main predator.

Life once again began to take on a better light for Soledad. She and Alberto continued to see each other openly and they enjoyed a lovely and intense romance with the blessing and consent of her mother. Meanwhile he worked hard and barely had time to practice his only known hobby, hunting with his rifle, a sport where he stood out as an excellent hunter and sharp shooter.

"Do you consider it to be a capital sin to stop Don Justi´s abuses at once and at any cost?" confessed Soledad to Alberto one day in desperation and with tears in her eyes. "What should I do?" She had already told him everything that was going on between the monster and her, and shocking him even more with her howls, she added: "It is just not fair that this man should continue to harm any woman he takes a fancy to. It is not right that there is no law to protect us, nor a political or religious authority to look after us."

"My life is a continuous torment just because this abusive pig goes around unpunished," she continued, as she shed inconsolable tears.

"If I didn't have my little daughter, I would have poisoned the bastard a long time ago," she said, adding in desperation, "How can you help me?"

After taking a long while to absorb the shock of such a tantalizing confession Alberto wondered "Yes, why not? I could easily give her some of my chemical products and let her take her revenge," but being a religious, simple and uncomplicated man, he answered painfully: "But that is not right my dear Soledad. I understand and dearly lament how much you are suffering, but it is not Christian to even think of killing someone, no matter how cruel he or she is towards you and others. No one has the right to take anyone else's life. You need to calm down and let me think how I should handle this situation," and he wondered again:

"Why does it take so long for justice and the new order to arrive, when it has already been proclaimed by the government to be imposed throughout the country?"

Alberto had made the big mistake of letting his support for independence be known, and also he had also confidentially made some derogatory comments about his patron's prolific family. What a miscalculation! On top of this he was naïve enough to think that, after talking to Peta about his intention to marry her daughter and adopt her little girl, and letting the landlord know about his wedding proposal, this would be welcome: he could not have been more wrong.

"What wonderful news, my dear doctor Yupanqui! Was the hypocritical comment of the dirty swine "You both deserve the best of this world and ought to be happy." "However," he added caressing his untidy beard and pretending to be concerned, "this ferocious plague that I have just got news of, that has recently appeared in our high lands, needs your urgent attention before it spreads out of control, doctor Yupanqui. So, very unfortunately, we will have to postpone your intentions until after your return."

The foxy son of a bitch was quick and had just fabricated a pretext with the sole idea of somehow, and without any scruple, getting rid of the young professional; and from this very moment he started to work on his sinister plan.

"One day all these abuses will be over and will be a thing of the past," thought Alberto while riding his horse alone close to the dangerous precipices of the Andean range, on his way to the high lands. He did not fully believe the pretext given by Don Justi, or in his supposedly good intentions either. As a result he was riding extremely carefully, particularly when approaching dangerous spots. "This Don Justi has neither flag nor God and is capable of anything to achieve his dirty purposes," he mused.

Sure enough, when rounding a tight corner high in the Andes, his horse got nervous and refused to go forward. It only advanced when Alberto pressed the spurs on its haunches and the horse stepped with its full weight onto a precarious plank; neighing with terror, it plunged into the void of a precipice. Alberto, in desperation, lurched off the horse's back and managed to grab hold of a tree branch that was prodigiously hanging far out over the cliff edge and miraculously saved his life; but nothing else, not his horse, nor the food, nor any thing else that he had brought along.

Convinced that this accident could not be a simple misfortune but that mysterious hands had changed the planks for rotten ones, Alberto decided to abandon his endeavour. For two days with no food or shelter, he walked all the way back down to Agallpampa, closer to the coast.

The origins of the sexual licentiousness to procreate freely and irresponsibly were an ancient Iberian practice that had somehow got revived in Spanish America. Although not written in any text of law, it existed as an ancient custom called *"derecho de pernada"*, which was nothing less than the right of the land owner to deflower the bride of any marriage held on his land. In other words, it was the patron who had the right to spend the first night with the bride immediately after the wedding ceremony, before even the groom,.

It was a cruel and abusive habit that was deeply rooted and widely accepted, even by the wife of the culprits. A custom that somehow contradicted the mandate of the Catholic Church that the bride had to arrive at her wedding a virgin; but to whose benefit?

In the Incas' age, however, before the Europeans arrived, there had existed a custom far advanced for its time: called "Servinacuy" or trial marriage, a bride and a groom would cohabit together for as long as they wanted, until they made sure that they understood each other and were compatible: otherwise they separated amicably and continued their lives as if nothing had happened, even if the "trial" wife got pregnant. This sexual liberty, contrary to the western formal marriage, shows how differently the Incas used to see life.

The first night sleeping in the open was not easy for Alberto; not from the lack of equipment or experience, or desire to rest - he had plenty of that - but from a gut feeling that he was being stalked. He spent a long and sleepless night, alert and laying on his back. He was tense and with his eyes wide open like an owl, his right hand holding his knife under his poncho, waiting for something, anything, to happen.

Midnight passed and suddenly he felt as if somebody was hidden by the trees, crouching and slowly approaching him. He waited, holding his breath until the last second until the shadow threw itself upon him violently. In a flash, he rolled over and out of the way, avoiding the blade of the knife that was furiously impaled into the grass where he had been just a few seconds before. His immediate reaction was to grab the hand of his aggressor, which gave him the upper hand in the struggle that followed. Alberto began stabbing his assailant repeatedly and, before finishing him off, managed to get a confession from him: he had been sent by Don Justi.

"We will fight to the last man! These coastal bastards cannot defeat us, and along with God and the king of Spain we will prevail. We are informed that a military column is approaching Kon Kon, and should be upon us by late afternoon tomorrow." This was the assessment of the situation pronounced by Don Justi, the leader of the rebels and president of the defence committee urgently assembled to defend the town from the imminent attack.

An assault that they knew well in advance was going to come sooner or later, since they dared to defy insolently the legal Constitution of the Republic and had maintained the region faithful to the Spanish Crown, against all odds. That was the reason why almost all the rich land owners of the area were present and why they were well prepared to repel any possible attempt to subdue them.

It was early 1832, almost eleven years after the declaration of independence, and Otuzco, a small village of no more than two thousand inhabitants, was very nervous and ebullient that day. Don Justiniano Herrera and other notable citizens from hundreds of miles around, among them big shots like Mayor Rodrigo Carranza, Jose Carlos Gamarra and Juan Francisco de Orbegoso had come together in the town hall to fight for their lives; or to fight for their life style, to be more exact. All of them were ultra-royalists and some were well known obnoxious individuals such as Don Justi. Strangely, among them there were a few correct, but misinformed, citizens. They discussed strategies and what they had to do to defend their so-called sacred cause.

Among those assembled - he could not be absent of course - was the priest "el cojo" Esquerre. "Cojo" in Spanish means a one legged man, but although he had both of his inferior members, he obtained the nickname because he limped. He was the vicar, as well as sole owner, of a large country estate called "La Mariquita". Curiously, among the defenders nobody remembered or seemed not to remember how Esquerre had became the one and only owner of such a prestigious and awesome estate.

"El Cojo" had a succulent and picturesque history. It was said by old timers that everything began with the arrival of Emilio Vidal, a lowlander who came to work as an accountant at "La Mariquita", many years before Esquerre.

"La Mariquita" was the name of the immense estate that used to be owned by Dona Aurora Peña and had been, for generations, in the hands of her family. She was a well preserved widow in her late sixties; however Vidal fell in love with her and they lived together happily in an unofficial sort of marriage for a long time. That was until Father Esquerre arrived on the scene with a pale young fellow as his assistant to take care of the parish of that vast territory. Esquerre first became Dona Aurora's confessor and later her lover.

It was obvious and commented on by all that there was a homosexual relationship between the priest and the young man, so this love affair, instead of being a love triangle, was actually more like a love quadrangle.

One night, tired of the priest's unfaithfulness, one of them - nobody ever discovered who - paid a gang to rough up the priest, stuff his unconscious body into a sack, and throw it over the wall onto his parish patio as if it were a sack of potatoes. It was necessary to re-assemble the poor man like a jigsaw puzzle; it took him months to pull through, although he never recovered the full use of his left leg.

The priest's revenge though took some time to mature; then it was slow but lethal; his two possible enemies disappeared from the face of the earth without leaving the slightest trace. Then, mysteriously, the widow's time arrived and after a short illness that lasted no more than a few months. Nobody knows how but the priest became the sole owner of such a large property, with the deeds of the property duly signed in his favour.

By late afternoon on April 11th, 1832, the town of Otuzco was totally surrounded by Republican troops; they were eager to punish this insignificant part of the country that still dared to challenge the Constitutional Government. An officer in full uniform and holding a white flag in his right hand stood in front of the town hall's main door presenting an ultimatum to the Mayor, demanding the immediate surrender of the town and complete subjugation to the Constitution. If they did not obey the order, the defenders would have to pay the consequences.

Otuzco was the administrative, political and social meeting point of the large land lords of the area; some of them living as far as two and even three days distance by horseback. The Royalists were convinced that independence was not possible in a country like Peru. But more than anything else, of course, they were defending their extremely comfortable way of life and were ready to die for that cause.

"We are a peaceful and very religious people, obedient to the Royal Laws governing these lands and will not surrender: we will not obey anybody but our king. In God's name and on behalf of our lord the King of Spain, we demand the immediate withdrawal of all your troops from our land," said the tough written response handed over by a nervous Don Justi.

The rebels were confident that they could repel any possible Republican attack by door-to-door fighting through the system of barricades they had strategically set up. More than anything else though, they were counting heavily on reinforcement, supposedly from the decimated and hungry troops of the Royalist General Rodriguez who were still at large somewhere in the mountains; they had sent messages urging Rodriguez to come to their assistance.

"We have enough provisions to resist for a month, but in less than two or three weeks General Rodriguez's troops will arrive, reinforced by extra troops supplied by our dear landlords". This was the assessment made by the sergeant, head of the reduced and drunkard gendarmerie posted in Otuzco; the royalists had bribed him to their cause and irresponsible given him accountability for defending the plaza.

"Once they arrive," the intoxicated officer continued,

slurring his wishful thinking "we should have the Republicans surrounded. We will shoot at them at will, from two different directions, wiping them off the map for good."

By night time, however, the snipers of the Republican troops had already been stationed in strategic positions behind the rocks and trees of the mountains surrounding the town. Among them was an anxious but resolute young man thirsty for justice, who had joined the troops when passing through Agallpampa, and had volunteered to guide them through the mountain's passages. Alberto Yupanqui had more personal and sublime reasons than any of his new comrades in arms as his motivations were love and vengeance as well as patriotism. He was coming for Soledad and Elisa, her little girl, and probably, just as important, he was coming to settle personal accounts with Justi.

From the early hours of the next day, the order to attack the town was imminent. By this time Alberto knew where Don Justi was staying, and impatiently waited for the order. When this was given, somewhere around midday, the shooting started and the unstoppable Republican troops initiated their advance inch by inch towards the Plaza de Arms, the neuralgic centre of the town.

After about two hours of bitter and bloody infighting, the troops unrelentingly continued advancing, trench by trench, in spite of the ferocious and heroic resistance of the locals. The women, children and old folk were hiding under their beds waiting in a panic for the outcome of this barbarous dispute.

To everyone's surprise, the Republicans suddenly began to fall, one after another - shot in the back as they hadn't seen the stealthy enemy coming up from behind; it was obvious that the long awaited reinforcements for the Royalists had arrived on time; it seemed that the tables had turned in the locals favour.

A euphoric Don Justi, together with two companions

also inflamed by the news being transmitted by the look outs stationed on the nearby church towers, emerged from the town hall crouching and looking apprehensively at each side of the street. They started to advance slowly towards the next trench, to reinforce the lines. All three were carrying double barrel rifles at the ready and across their chests they wore wide belts full of extra bullets.

They advanced carefully, their backs against the wall, still looking around nervously, their eyes scanning first one side, then the other. They had not gained two yards before Don Justi´s barrel figure was already moving into Alberto's rifle's range.

Meanwhile the arrival of mass reinforcements for the locals turned out to be a short lived false alarm: the individuals shooting at the Republicans from behind, were identified as a small bunch of diehard Royalists from a nearby *hacienda,* folk who paid dearly for their daring action: they were exterminated like rabbits by the incensed Republicans.

"This is for Soledad... this one is for little Elisa... this for Peta... and this one for a new Peru" Alberto murmured while calmly pulling the trigger of his rifle, allowing the bullets to escape their chamber at slow intervals, one by one, as though he were enjoying it; as if revenge was a dish to be eaten luxuriously, and enjoyed very slowly, bite by bite. The heavy body of "Don Justi" seemed to take flight and, as if in slow motion slid towards the ground, landing as a bloody mangled mess, with nothing left to show of the power that this man had taken for granted his entire life.

Later on, people speculated that the tyrant had been killed by bullets emanating from different rifles, and that a few of the shots might even have been fired by some of his own children. However, the truth is that the two individuals with him, who were also mortally wounded, were his sons.

A cannon had to be used to blast one of the towers of the venerable Church of her Beloved Holiness, known by the locals as "The Virgin of the Door", to put an end to the bloody battle. The tower collapsed in an explosion of rubble and dust, to the outcry of the religious and frightened population already out on the streets demanding an end to the struggle: to stop this ugly, fraternal and sacrilegious battle that was now destroying one of the heirlooms of their faith.

The town was overtaken over by a mob that streamed out from the houses looking desperately for their fighting relatives, and crying and screaming when finding them dead or badly injured. Some were greeting and cheering the Republican as their saviours. Among this confusion the military operations were over by around five in the afternoon.

Some people used the confusion of the moment to settle personal accounts: among the corpses found in the town hall was that of "Cojo" Esquerre's, with his testicles stuffed in his mouth. By the end, more than one hundred and fifty-four people had lost their lives and many more were seriously wounded.

After the battle of Otuzco, Soledad and Alberto, together with little Elisa, decided to leave the Chuquibamba *hacienda* and to go beyond the mountains as far as possible from that detested place. For months and months they walked and trekked by mule further inland, eastward towards the rain forest, looking for the ideal place where the land had no owners and no tyrants. Finally, when they found the plot of land they liked, they proclaimed it theirs; they had established themselves in the Amazon Jungle. Later on the family raised eight offspring and their farm grew to become a prosperous estate.

PART III

PAPA LUCHO

"Paca" was terrified as she huddled in the amphibious vehicle minutes before the massive and awesome invasion began. Hundreds of thousands of troops poured from the amphibious vehicles, with the enraged roaring of fighter planes flying overhead. The noise and mayhem that greeted the soldiers made it seem as though they were stepping into the end of the world. Strangely, "Paca" found that her fear left her and was replaced by an eerie feeling of calmness as she entered the middle of the apocalyptic pandemonium which was Normandy on June 06, 1944.

In spite of the explosions and the canon shots fired at the Allied Invasion Force by the frantic Nazi defences; and notwithstanding the blinding and blazing smoke, the mud, the dust and the pieces of dismembered human bodies flying in the air, "Paca" was unruffled. This was probably because she was a survivor; she had become used to attacks, along with the mayhem they produced, from an early age, when in her remote tribe near Iquitos – a hectic and ebullient town on the left bank of the remote Amazon river - where her tribe was accustomed to attacks from their enemies and the loss of family members and friends.

"Paca", petite and vivacious, was probably the first Peruvian jungle native to serve under the British flag. She was not a beautiful young woman by any standards, but she was attractive and sensual enough to drive British men her age 'crazy'; her lascivious and exotic personality, free of any conventional inhibitions, gave her a tremendous sex appeal. Or to put it simply: "Paca" had the wild sexual drive typical of the nature and temperament of jungle people.

She got involved in the war for two reasons. First, because she was in love with a young army doctor called Frank Lee. Secondly, because like so many of her colleges in the Middlesex Hospital, where she was working as a nurse, she had been hypnotized with passion and patriotism when listening to Winston Churchill's harangues on the radio and decided to volunteer for the war effort, although she was under no obligation whatsoever to serve in the Armed Forces.

"Many of my male and female colleges from the hospital were drafted and some of us decided to join the army voluntarily," she informed the Peruvian Consul in Berlin months later.

She had found the Consul, alone and famished due to food shortages in the devastated city, sitting in a ruined and derelict building. He had been astonished when Paca, still in a British lieutenant's uniform, walked into his office having made a dangerous journey through the rubble of the almost flattened city during the wettest and coldest winter on record in the early stage of the occupation of Germany. She didn't feel like telling him that she had volunteered because she couldn't tolerate living so far away from her beloved boyfriend, who, sadly, was one of the first allied casualties to die at Dunkirk.

Once back and nursing again in London, Paca confided her personal story to her room mate in their flat at 60 Nassau Street, beside the Middlesex Hospital, when she was feeling nostalgic. "My mother was a maid who nursed her patron, "Papa Lucho", when he was extremely ill a few years before he died in Iquitos. My mother had to travel urgently to our village and so I was sent to replace her. For me, sixteen at that time, it was a great honour, as the patient was a well known and loved person, as well as honest and famous for being fair and he treated his workers well.

These workers were counted by the thousands. I knew that he was immensely wealthy, but I didn't know that he was suffering from malaria. I only knew that he was in distress and badly in need of attention, and I was more than glad to do anything for him; I had some experience from attending my own father before he passed away."

"Then," she continued, "the old man recovered and he was so grateful for the care I had given him that he called my mother to tell her, "I owe so much to this girl and I would like to pay for it."

"She wants to be a nurse and I would like her to be a real one".

"What would you think of me paying for her nursing studies in London?" proposed Don Lucho.

"For my mother it seemed that her daughter was being given the opportunity of a life time; but she was so ignorant, she probably thought London was just around the corner, or as far away as Lima. Almost everyone in Iquitos only knew Lima from photographs."

In that remote town of Iquitos, so far removed from civilization, not just for Paca's mother but for everyone living in that "nest of river pirates", it was like being invited to visit Mars. Nevertheless, her mother agreed with the idea and against all the odds Paca set off on her journey; finally, after sailing endlessly for close to two months in a steamer belonging to the "Booth Line" of Liverpool, she reached the United Kingdom. The liner frequently operated the route Iquitos, Manaus and the British port, carrying that highly prized and highly valuable commodity called rubber.

"Papa Lucho" was the nickname of Don Luis Morey Arias, a very wealthy rubber baron operating in the heart of the immense Amazon rain forest. Iquitos was a remote, almost inaccessible small community. From Lima it was impossible to reach it overland, no matter how many months or maybe even years you had at your disposal. Should you approach it from Europe, after crossing the Atlantic you still had to penetrate the Amazon River mouth on the Atlantic Ocean and then navigate up river for weeks, even months, through inhospitable, mysterious and very dangerous jungle.

Because of this, right up until the beginning of the XX century it was easier for wealthy parents in Iquitos to send their children to study in Europe than in Lima. The Amazon River was, and still is, the vital artery connecting this impenetrable and never-ending gigantic part of the jungle. And that is precisely how Don Luis Morey Cab de Bou, a young and fearless Spanish adventurer from Majorca and father of "Papa Lucho", arrived in this remote area at the beginning of the nineteenth century.

Don Luis was altogether a different sort of Spanish conqueror, very different from the rest of his predecessors. He didn't want to make his fortune in the old way; he was an unusual breed of explorer who wanted to establish himself somewhere that those before him would not have dared to settle, in the heart of the Peruvian Amazon Jungle. So he left his beautiful island, as well as his beloved family and went off, against all the rational odds, into the unknown, to that far-flung and exotic country; it was only a few years after most Spaniards had left Peru following independence from Spain.

Curiously, Don Luis was not trying to avoid danger; on the contrary, he was looking for it. He had pondered his decision over and over again and took a calculated risk. "To reach Iquitos from the Pacific Ocean is not an impossible task; it can be reached after a hazardous non-stop trip on horseback through breathtaking scenery, with dangerous mountain passages, enduring freezing temperatures past the high peaks of the Andes and infernal heat when you descend into the rain forest. Then one has to paddle by canoe through malaria-infested swamps and inhospitable marshes, always battling the cursed mosquitoes for months before finally, if you survive to tell the tale, arriving at Iquitos".

Instead of taking this comparatively safer journey, Don Luis, being a more gallant sort of explorer, decided for the longer, more hazardous alternative. He would cross the Atlantic first and then penetrate the mouth of the frightening Amazon River from the opposite direction up river; he was not sure where his final destination would be, only that this way would be far more challenging, with plenty of adventures and risks to be taken.

So after facing incredible sacrifices through the dangerous territory of a dense and impenetrable jungle replete with venomous snakes, reptiles and unknown animals and inhabited by lethal head-hunters, and hostile cannibal tribes, he arrived at Iquitos.

After only a few months there, he came to the conclusion that it was not to his liking, so he decided to push his luck and keep on going inland, west of Iquitos, until he ended up in Tarapoto. This was a rural community set in the eastern foot hills of the Andes. He had made an amazing two thousand, one hundred mile trip inland from the Amazon's mouth; finally he had found the environment he was looking for.

Tarapoto was a tiny outpost, a minuscule hamlet located where "the devil lost his poncho", as the natives said when referring to an extremely remote and isolated place. In time this unassuming settlement would become the humble nest where, in 1870, the great "Papa Lucho" was born, from the marital union of Don Luis with the beautiful Elisa Yupanqui Bracamonte, the mature daughter of one Soledad Bracamonte, the adopted daughter of a pioneering and wealthy farmer named Alberto Yupanqui.

"Papa Lucho" didn't have to inherit his natural instincts for adventure and entrepreneurship from anyone. Since early childhood he had navigated the River Huallaga on his own as well as up and down other tributaries of the Amazon, which so fascinated him. Caiman hunting and trading almost anything imaginable with the natives along the river banks was his business, and that is how he became fluent in several native languages.

Moaning and groaning, the decrepit steamer indolently rounds a corner of the pleasant river and made its way down the great River Huallaga, surroundered by the dramatic lush vegetation of gargantuan and millenarian trees. "Papa Lucho" has already spent a week in this humid and sticky heat, and has barely reached Nauta, even though the navigation is down river.

They still have to endure another week to Iquitos which is the boat's final destination. Everybody on board, male and female, travel literally piled on top of each other in the overcrowded ferry among a cargo of tapioca, banana, and other exotic fruits, and with live chickens, pigs and a few baby monkeys.

Throughout this hellish voyage of insupportably high temperatures and stormy, tropical rain, they all travel almost naked. At night time when it gets fresher, a different sort of torment appears: the vicious mosquitoes. In spite of the overcrowded conditions, or precisely because of it, travellers gave free rein to their sexual desires.

It's an airless mosquito-clouded afternoon and young Luis Morey lies in his hammock. A strikingly good-looking man who is trying hard to concentrate on the conjugation of the verb 'to be', as he is learning English with the solitary help of a badly worn-out textbook, he is almost close to memorizing the entire manuscript.

Apart from the book, all his thoughts are now focused on the rubber trade, as he has decided to get into that business no matter what; since he has heard of the immense amount of money one can make if ready to make the sacrifice of going into the jungle for months at a time, something that is not unusual for him. But he doesn't want just to apply for that job; he wants to have an edge over the innumerable number of other applicants. He wants to be fluent in English so he can deal direct with the British traders. He is a tall young man of a white complexion, dark hair and clear eyes in a handsome face, with an imposing muscular figure.

After sexually servicing a young female passenger, who seems to be always in need, the boat's captain, smiling and buttoning up his shirt, comes out of his cabin and approaches Luis's hammock to ask: "Do you really believe Papa Lucho that it is true these foreign traders are paying as much money as people say for rubber? That there are Peruvians who are therefore making a bundle?"

The captain is addressing the young man using the familiar name that everybody knows him by: "Papa" or Dad, in spite of the fact that he is only a little more than 18 years old. This is out of respect and admiration for his audacity and boldness when starting an enterprise, any endeavour in fact, in addition to his "bonhomie" and paternalism.

"It seems to be true, but you have to be prepared to surrender your freedom for a really long time. On top of that you need to be fluent in their language if you want to do business directly with them," was Luis Morey's honest answer, while fastidiously shooing the mosquitoes away from his mouth.

"Papa Lucho" is going down river in precisely the opposite direction his father had when he came to Peru 30 years beforehand, although they both were pursuing the same goal: to have adventures and at the same time to make their fortunes.

The old man had been able to leave a sizable fortune to his only son when he passed away, a considerable part of which Papa Lucho is now carrying along with him to be invested in this venture, as ingots of gold sewn into the interior part of his clothes. He is the only one among the passengers wearing the typical paraphernalia explorers use in the jungle: a hard hat, a patch-pocketed jacket, a pair of high boots, a machete and the never-absent Colt 45 pistol.

"I only want my chance to win the trust of these people" This is how Papa always refers to the business he was getting into. "And that will be the basis on which I will build an empire" Although an unassuming man, he was cocksure about his future success.

It has been raining hard for several days and the "Practico" has problems seeing through the dense curtain of water formed by the torrential downpour, so the creaky old steamer slows down and moors up on one side of the river, as it is extremely dangerous to continue without the professional guidance of a "Practico".

The "Practico" is one of the most important members of the crew: it is he who keeps an eye on the river conditions, also checking from time to time the position of the stars. He is a knowledgeable man - always a native - in charge of showing the way the vessel should go: he signals instructions to the helmsman with his hands as to how to avoid the sand banks, floating tree trunks and other hazards. He usually sits on the prow, with his feet hanging freely over the sides of the boat.

After years "Papa Lucho's dream had become reality and he made far more money than he had ever dreamed of. He created the Casa Morey, an extremely strong trading company with assets in England as well as in Peru. Through purchases and staking claims to land he obtained the whole left bank of the Amazon River between Iquitos and the Brazilian border, a mighty state of more than twenty million acres.

So Don Luis or "Papa Lucho" Morey was already one of the richest men in Peru, with a estimated net worth of six million pounds sterling - equivalent nowadays to one hundred million pounds sterling or two hundred million American dollars; he had amassed this though years of supplying "black gold", as the rubber bundles collected by an army of several thousand rainforest Indian used to be called.

As he used to say: "Everything is built on trust" – the trust the traders had in him and the trust he had in his people. He imposed on the jungle, and above all on that "nest of river pirates" the principle that you had to deliver what you promised, a completely unknown standard in that part of the world.

On one of his trips to Europe he became fascinated by the Eiffel Tower and managed to meet Mr. Eiffel personally. With a friend he commissioned the famous French engineer to build a house made out of steel , disassembled it bit by bit and had it packed and shipped to Iquitos, where it still stands today in the Main Square and is known as the "Iron House".

This was when the British started to build ships completely out of steel. A couple of them were commissioned by the Peruvian Government and sent to be assembled on Titicaca Lake, the highest navigable lake in the world at twelve thousand five hundred feet above sea level. Piece by piece the ships were transported by mule back over the daunting Andes. Instead of the six months that had been allowed to get the ships up and running on the lake, it took six solid years, and some of the British engineers died during the ordeal to finish the endeavour. Today one of those ships stands moored to a pier there, as a floating museum, ready to be operated again, thanks to the dedication and indefatigable effort of a British lady called Meriel Larken.

What a different history to that of Julio Cesar Arana, the other outstanding Peruvian Rubber Baron. When Papa Lucho was trying to get into this business, at the turn of the XIX century, another legendary jungle pioneer was already navigating the Huallaga, Ucayali and other rivers searching for *caucho* or rubber trees. This extraordinary young man was called Julio Cesar Arana, the son of an entrepreneurial businessman who had made a small fortune in the Panama-hat boom.

Julio Cesar, was a born leader and hailed from the little rain forest town of Rioja, located in the remote north east part of Peru, where the eastern Andean Cordillera begin their abrupt descent into the Amazon jungle. He was a strong man of medium stature and a commanding charisma with a dynamic and indomitable personality, a bit vain in his appearance but incredibly ambitious and audacious when it came to doing business. In other words he was a tough businessman, a real bulldozer.

Don Julio Cesar and Papa Lucho, were by far the two most formidable and towering Rubber Barons that Peru has ever known. They both belonged to the same generation, being born almost at the same time - Don Julio Cesar in 1864 and Papa Lucho in 1870, and in the same area, just sixty miles apart: the first in Rioja and the second in Tarapoto, two of the mildewed little jungle outposts on the left side of the River Huallaga. They both made fabulous fortunes through imposing and magnetic personalities, starting at the early age of eighteen.

Without knowing each other, early in life and in different ways they both decided to try their hands at making a fortune looking for the precious rubber. This commodity was on the verge of a boom, as the automobile industry was becoming insatiable in its demands for more and more rubber, and the Amazon rain forest was thick with it.

Julio Cesar Arana was always ahead of the game. By the time he was twenty he had already recruited a six hundred strong army of foremen who put the rain forest indigenous to work by the thousands. He ran a business from Iquitos in Peru to Manaus in Brazil, making them the two most important rubber cities in the world, cities that would drive the automobile into the industrial age.

By the turn of the century Julio Cesar had finessed enough leases and had staked enough claims to master the rubber rich Putumayo area, a large stretch of jungle of about twelve million acres. This, together with other claims, added up to a staggering total of almost twenty six million acres under his control.

These two mighty colossi made Iquitos – a jungle outpost unreachable by land - one of the richest cities on the planet. Julio Cesar and Papa Lucho were both running empires from their mansions in Iquitos, the Casa Arana and the Casa Morey, which, due to their immense size and the ornamentation on their façades, resembled the Portuguese palaces they both liked and admired so much. They had lush gardens full of tropical plants and trees where exotic birds and animals roamed, and the flowering bougainvillea provided a rainbow of vibrant colours.

From their majestic balconies overlooking the mighty river they could proudly watch their barges approach packed with "black gold; the river was thick with steamers and barges, as well as thousands of people manning the operations under their command.

For the simple and uncomplicated inhabitants of Iquitos, who were also full of prejudices, superstitions and envy, all this led to the belief that the two tycoons had a *pacto con el Diablo,* a pact with the devil. This only added to the legend of these two extraordinary men.

Julio Cesar, always the leader, incorporated his business in New York and in London, then hired a British board of directors and listed it on the London Stock Exchange under the name of the Peruvian Amazon Company. The Casa Arana had the monopoly of the best quality rubber, the 'Para Fine' hard grade; at the same time it was creating an abominable inferno out of an otherwise idyllic and unspoiled piece of jungle.

It was revealed years later, to the world's horror, that hundreds of gunmen were scouring the jungle for slaves, sweeping the villages, terrorizing the Indians and herding the poor souls with false promises throughout the jungle trails to slavery.

When the full story of the atrocities committed by Casa Arana's people began to appear in papers and magazines world wide, the public were shocked at the macabre vision of Indians herded together at gun point; chained to one another, naked, to be sold to overseers for twenty to forty pounds sterling each; and then being forced to work simply to stay alive. It was revealed that the foremen were working on a commission basis, so the more rubber their people collected the more money they made and in order to make more money, they needed as many people as they could find.

The crimes committed by Arana's boys were unspeakable and beyond the cruellest imagination. Moreover, they appeared in the most reputable international publications, to such an extent that the good name of the Putumayo paradise, surrounded by pristine water falls and gorgeous rivers, was changed to "Devil's Paradise". Other revelations came to light: Indians were working without payment, without food, under terrible conditions, with women stolen, ravished and murdered; Indians were being flogged to death and their bodies used to feed the dogs; drunken evil foremen were shooting people just for the fun of it.

By the time the scandal surfaced, around three hundred thousand rain forest Indian had died, some due to starvation, some from acquired infectious diseases due to criminal negligence, and the rest had been executed for the pleasure and amusement of Arana's henchmen.

Julio Cesar Arana's empire finally collapsed due to the scandal. Its otherwise mighty shares disintegrated on the Stock Exchanges like ice melting into water, and its board of directors disbanded in shame, arguing that they knew nothing of the felony. So Julio Cesar, by then known as "the devil of the Putumayo", spent the rest of his days in voluntary solitary confinement in a little dwelling overlooking the Pacific Ocean on the outskirts of Lima.

He bequeathed to his children, relatives and many generations to come, the stigma of his name associated with the atrocities committed by his employees, no doubt with his consent; as if a morbid invisible rubberstamp were fixed on their forehead as the "Mark of Arana". Some relatives, unjustly victims of the scandal, had their assets frozen; it took years to liberate them, and indeed some never managed to do so at all.

Papa Llucho was certainly not a saint; his weak side was, and you might not blame him for that, women. In a way it was understandable in a man of his type. He was always on the move and far from home in a land well known for its promiscuity; he had to cope with the constant pestering of girls hungry to have children from such a good looking and wealthy stallion. "I would like a little boy" or "a little girl" were the too frequent "Orders" put on him, or sexual requests he had to deal with.

Later, in a moment of lucidity before he died, "Papa Lucho" said to his relatives: "One day in the not too distant future, all my wealth will disappear." Who knows, maybe as a result of abuses made by his people or maybe as revenge from the jungle, or just as a payback to the famous pact with the devil that people insisted he had made, the old man had a premonition; and so it happened: in less than two generations absolutely nothing was left of his enormous fortune.

Several years before the old man died, a sinister and penniless character appeared in Iquitos. A short man known as "Pichicho" Ismael, who, because he happened to be fluent in English, was taken on by "Papa Lucho" to work in his company as a broker, and stayed in that post for some time. He was well considered by the Morey Family and a frequent guest at the family's dinner table, but a few months before the old man passed away, he saw his opportunity.

He argued that he had advanced some of his own money, a huge amount of pounds sterling to some rubber contractors on behalf of "Papa Lucho", and he managed to lock the family in a long and nasty judicial case that lasted for thirty-six bloody years and ended up bankrupting the next generations of Moreys.

"I only came to this inferno to make money, which is what makes the world spin," Pichicho Ismael used to say in the gambling saloon of the Iquitos Social Club when he was drunk, which was most of the time. "Either you have money and are somebody, or you have nothing and are absolutely nobody; you choose." So this gold digger waited for the right moment and bam! His plot was engineered with his poker buddies at the Club, a bunch of good-for-nothing and envious individuals.

World War II was already over and after making the most of Europe, a disenchanted and homesick "Paca", now in her forties and decorated by the British Empire with the iron cross for bravery - for putting her life in danger under the Union Jack - unassumingly returned to Peru to live in Lima with the Morey family until the end of her days. Although she was not a relative, she was considered as such; contrary to other close members of the family who, after the Peruvian/Colombian war, were not recognised by the Moreys.

That war – one of the least remembered elsewhere in the world – had been caused by the Putumayo Trapezium, a big chunk of the Peruvian territory that had been owned by the Casa Arana; the North American government 'gave' it to Colombia, they say, as compensation for the territory they themselves had taken from that country to create the Republic of Panamá and build the Canal. In other words, the North Americans placated Colombian's claim with a territory that was not theirs.

The Morey family distanced themselves from their relatives in Putamayo supposing they had sold their big *hacienda,* a huge estate called Leticia, to the Colombian enemies, and as a result were considered traitors to their country. The *hacienda* that had been sold was precisely the part that had been bequeathed to the estranged family in "Papa Lucho's" last will.

Whatever the circumstance or whichever the deal, if in reality it existed, the United States appears granting a part of a foreign land as if it were theirs to give; most importantly for the winners, this deal gave away something invaluable: free access to navigate the Amazon River, a strategic key in that remote part of the world, and ironically now, one of the main routes for the cocaine traffic.

The war was just another pantomime in South American history, although a sad and expensive one: it cost the lives of a number of valiant soldiers from both sides; Peru, once again, gained a few more "military heroes" whose names they could use to name streets in towns throughout the country, as well as constructing military monuments wholesale, as they have always done.

ECONOMIC MIGRATION, 1910

The shimmering sands stretched out before them; the day was warm and calm, immense sand dunes, palms and carob trees were spread out over the desert floor near the city of Trujillo, breaking the monotony of the green and grey-blue scenery. To the north-east, one could see the imposing outlines of the hills that form the western range of the Andes.

The riders advanced at a trot, with the elegant and singular gait that the Peruvian 'Paso' horse has, swinging its forelegs airily from side to side. Who knows when these descendants of the famous Berber horses learned by some quirk of nature to move in such a peculiar way, producing the smoothest ride a horseman can possibly have.

There were about thirty '*chalanes*', as riders were called here, who advanced in a long single line, keeping abreast of one another to avoid throwing dust up at each other as they rode. Behind them, cargo mules carried their personal belongings. All of them wore light straw hats with a wide brim, worn down over their eyebrows; without exception they all wore cream or white clothing. Some of them, like Don Miguel Del Mar, leader of the caravan, wore a linen poncho that was thrown over one shoulder, bandoleer style.

The entourage was made up of Don Miguel Del Mar and his sons, together with twenty-six friends who had volunteered to help them establish themselves on a new piece of land further north, near Trujillo. At six in the morning they were leaving the Virú Valley to enter the desert that lay between there and the Moche Valley. They had left Chorobal, closer to the sierra, the previous morning and spent the night in the town of Virú. They were now ready for the last leg of their journey and planned to reach their destination by dusk.

Nobody spoke: it was a melancholy procession. Don Miguel and his four sons rode in the middle of the line. Robust and strong, they were the hardworking product of this fierce land. The youngest of the Del Mar family and of the group was Manuel, who at twelve years of age was already an accomplished rider. Their rugged, sunburned faces were etched with deep lines that looked as though they had been carved out with a chisel. Tears rolled down some of their cheeks.

Why were there no women in the family party? Nobody dared to speak, or ask questions. This was because they all knew the answer: they were accompanying Don Miguel to help him begin a new life. He was a man renowned for his honesty and integrity, highly respected in his community. For this reason they would accompany him to Trujillo or to the ends of the earth if it were necessary, without him needing to ask. Each one of them, in one way or another, owed a debt of gratitude to the Del Mar family.

For many months, since Dona Rosita's death, his partner of twenty-four years, Don Miguel had no longer been himself. He had stopped working with his usual dedication and tenderness. He was no longer attached to his land or his animals and was in danger of withdrawing into himself completely. Fortunately, he overcame his depression with the support of Rodrigo, his eldest son, who was now eighteen. Don Miguel had travelled to Trujillo with him to buy a plot of land between Moche and Salaverry, which he nostalgically named after the place they were leaving behind, his beloved Chorobal. With four young sons to raise Don Miguel felt he needed to be closer to civilisation.

The other men were accompanying them as protection

against highwaymen. Although the five Del Mar men formed a formidable shooting squad as it was, they did not wish to take unnecessary risks. Everyone they had left behind in the farm and the village had been tearful at their departure, because they felt a part of them was also painfully leaving. For Don Miguel and his sons, the pain was even greater, as they had lost their mother and now they were leaving their friends, their land, everything.

Before sundown, as they descended a hill, they spotted the plot of land and their future farm house. The silhouettes of the huge adobe 'Pyramid of the Sun' and 'Pyramid of the Moon' appeared on their right. These pyramids had been built to honour the Sun God and his wife almost a millennium beforehand by an extinct civilisation whose blood, in large or small proportions, ran through every one of the travellers. Below and to the left, they could see the port of Salaverry, where the Customs post had recently been moved after centuries of being located in Huanchaco, the bay where the first Spanish families had arrived and where some Viceroys had landed.

Don Miguel remembered his grandfather saying that his ancestors had always lived in Trujillo and the surrounding area, and that their origins had been in Huanchaco. Trujillo was where many generations, following the first Del Mar, had established themselves. He vaguely remembered that the old man had spoken of an 'Alvaro' who had come from Spain, doubtless some colonial adventurer or perhaps the scion of a noble house.

But his most famous and beloved ancestor was without doubt Don Simón, Alvaro's grandson, who had lost the family fortune. It was said this was due to an unnecessary confrontation with the Inquisition over his liberal ideas and contrary views. He had been warned on various occasions, but the stubborn old man refused to change his beliefs. He read many prohibited books and ended by being burned at the stake; his properties were confiscated and the only thing he left behind was two adult sons.

It was already night time when they arrived at the entrance to the dusty path that led to the little farm house. Tired, sweating and filthy, they dismounted, unloaded the mules and unsaddled the horses. Some of them still had the strength to make something hot to eat from the food rations that they carried, and as there was not enough room in the little house for them all, most of the group camped under the open sky.

The first days were not difficult. They enlarged the house, cleared the fields and prepared stables and farmyards. Gradually, and in small groups, the loyal escorts took their leave to begin their long ride home, satisfied with their accomplished mission. There was no question of money changing hands. Don Miguel and his sons thanked them all with a big hug wishing them luck and a safe journey.

Five men who are united in their purpose can perform miracles. By the end of a year Chorobal had flourished into a beautiful farm, an oasis between the sandy earth and the sea, where sugar cane, peanuts, sweet potatoes, vegetables and diverse fruit grew. The boys returned to school "because we must tame these colts", said Don Miguel. The exception was Rodrigo, who decided to stay at home to help his father.

In the summer the farm was a paradise for the children, who hunted ducks on the pond or fished off the beach after helping in the fields and at home. For deep sea fishing they used *caballitos de totora*, 'reed horses', as the Chimús had done thousands of years before. They rode these solid canoes that were made from reeds roped tightly together, with the pointed prows lifted out of the water like the tip of a clown's shoe and a straight, squared-off stern. They stored their fishing gear and their catch in the dip in the centre of the boat, which also served as a place to stand and surf the waves.

The years passed by in this tranquil setting. Fate was good to Don Miguel as he met and fell in love with Isabel

Saldaña, eighteen years his junior. They married and had many children. By the year 1918 life was good and generous for the Del Mar family, until one fateful day when they were testing the press designed by Rodrigo to extract sugar from cane. A piece of cane clogged the gears of the machine, while the team of oxen moving the mechanism continued round the axle. Rodrigo jumped up onto the press and tried to remove the cane when a curdling blood scream cut into the evening like a knife through Don Miguel's heart. The youngster fainted and collapsed into a pool of blood, his left arm severed by the machine that he and his father had built with such hope.

Dona Isabel had been playing with her son Fernando when she ran desperately to the place from where the scream emerged, finding a pale Don Miguel on his knees wrapping his son with his own shirt. The second eldest son jumped onto his horse and galloped away to Salaverry to ask for a small railway car to be sent urgently. Miraculously, in spite of the un-containable haemorrhage, Rodrigo recuperated and eventually went back to work. The one who took years to recover, if he ever did, was Don Miguel: it was just too much for him to accept that his eldest son, perhaps the kindest and most hard-working of them all, had become handicapped at such a young age.

Better years and prosperity followed. Around this time Don Miguel acquired a carriage that was pulled by fine horses and it was one of the few that existed in Trujillo. These were heady times for the city, when Progress Street, later Pizarro Street, was paved with English paving stones brought as ballast on the merchant ships trading guano.

The Del Mar family bought a house in Salaverry and another in Trujillo, one and a half blocks from the Plaza de Armas and around the corner from his friend Don Pedro de Bracamonte, a descendant of the Marquis de Herrera. The family grew and soon there were six new members. The older sons became independent and left their paternal home except for Rodrigo, who continued to work very closely with his father.

Trujillo, with its Marquises, Counts and Royal Constables, was still a serene and clean city with large colonial houses and sixty thousand inhabitants. Emperor Charles V and Queen Joanna of Castile had given the city the envied status of 'noble city' a long time before such a coat of arms had been conceded to Lima.

During the time of Independence from the Spaniards Trujillo had been provisionally declared as the capital of the Republic; Congress was held in Señora Urquiaga's house on Progress Street. People on foot and on horseback, with frock coat and hat, would pass along its cobbled streets, their gracious carriages and buggies contrasting with the carts drawn by work horses, and with the slow donkeys that transported the milk and fish of the barefoot vendors.

The ancient walls that still encircled the city and had defended her for centuries continued to yield to urban growth. Salaverry was a small port with a thousand souls at the time, with pretty wooden houses painted in different bright colours; sitting on the shores of a bay at the foot of a sandy stone hill. This small town lived by the rhythm imposed by its vibrant dock, where local and foreign vessels lay at anchor.

Both passengers and cargo all travelled by sea, this being the best way to reach Lima and other coastal cities. Travel overland by mule, the choice of a few brave merchants, was a daring trip of defiance. The train was still in its infancy and only connected Trujillo with the port of Salaverry and other large *haciendas* and villages of the Chicama River Valley.

It was here at the beginning of the 20th century that Fernando, Don Miguel's eldest son from his second wife, was raised in the isolated environment of the farm. He must have been six years old when he visited Trujillo for the first time. That memory, however, stayed with him as the day that he visited another world. He would never forget the first time he laid eyes on the enormous, palatial rooms of the Bracamonte mansion, with their solemn paintings and enormous ornamental mirrors, and how, painfully shy and dying of apprehension, he was afraid to walk on the valuable carpets.

The family carriage and the railway that passed near the farm gave them access to other customs and people, breaking the isolation in which they lived. Unfortunately, they would pay a very high price for this step into modernity as it was through these means of communication that death and desolation arrived. Some say that the plague entered the area through Salaverry, others that it was from other ports that received ships from the Orient. However it arrived, the feared bubonic plague cruelly decimated the population. One by one the del Mars watched their family members succumb to this terrible disease, among them their beloved Rodrigo; but the epidemic had a preference for the most vulnerable, the children. Of their nine children, only four survived.

Years later, Fernando would explain to his children how the little ones who were affected would be playing carefree and then suddenly become sad and isolate themselves. On examination, the black spots of death and swollen glands would show that nothing could be done for them. At the beginning, they would take sufferers to the medical post, but they were only sent home. There was simply no cure and one could only pray and wait for the call of death.

By 1924, Fernando, in spite of his tender age, had become a mature man at twelve. He was one of the countless anonymous heroes who had become accustomed to living with the death of their loved ones. He was no longer afraid of death and he had cried all his tears. He did not care that he could be the next victim; his only desire was to be useful to his family and to those who are dying around him. There was no more medicine in the region, or food, or transport: anything.

Even though he was tormented by sadness, Don Miguel continued to make his land produce crops, even though he lacked seeds and fertilisers. In spite of the desperate situation in which they found themselves, the family did not allow their dead to be buried without dignity and insisted it had to be in a coffin and in the cemetery. As there were no funeral companies or carpenters that could keep up with the overwhelming demand for coffins, Fernando had to chop up the dividing stalls of the stables, gently smoothing the wood while heavy tears cascaded down his cheeks and dampened his work. One by one, he manufactured coffins for his loved ones and inadvertently this is how he became a carpenter, alone, with no guidance, out of necessity and out of love.

When the worst was over and the family finished mourning their dead, a short period of happiness and wealth followed. With the help of his surviving children, Don Miguel rebuilt Chorobal and Dona Isabel gave birth to two more children before dying prematurely at forty- three years old.

Don Miguel was a widower once again. Already feeling his age he could no longer manage the farm alone. He missed his cherished Rodrigo and Fernando, his possible successor, was still too young and still studying. The problem worsened and Fernando found himself obliged to forgo his studies in order to help his family. He had only just finished at his primary school; Don Miguel accepted this situation as a temporary decision.

Don Miguel spent a lot of his time in Trujillo taking care of a pending court case involving unpaid debt. He had taken out a loan in order to raise pigs in large quantities, but they had all died due to the outbreak of devastating swine fever. Now he needed to reschedule the loan. The old patriarch defended his interests by retaining the services of a lawyer with a certain prestige in the city. What Don Miguel was trying to do was avoid being evicted from his farm - which he had offered as a guarantee for the loan - and he was now asking for a realistic time frame to honour his debt.

Fernando, at sixteen, was now responsible for the operation of the farm from dawn to dusk; he was also a substitute mother; he had to cook, see that the clothes and the house were clean and help his siblings with their homework. Day after day, night after night, year after year it was the same routine. For him, in his world - Chorobal - every day was the same. The harvests and the farm animals did not distinguish between Tuesday and Sunday.

Sundays were the only days off from school, and were the busiest day for this young man. Holidays were the same, as the children needed more attention. Curiously, this was not a problem for him. On the contrary, he felt such affection for his family and the land that he took care of his chores with pleasure.

At the beginning of the 1930s, Fernando, reading an old newspaper, discovered that a socialist revolution had begun in Trujillo. Other than combat planes flying overhead, nervous troops that passed by on the trains and an explosion here or there, the Del Mar family had had no idea that a student and workers uprising was under way that resulted in them taking over the army headquarters, shooting the officials and taking control of the city.

Their isolation was such that in spite of a distance of only twelve miles, they only heard of the details weeks later when Don Miguel acquired a radio in order to keep them more informed. Through the radio they heard that the rebel group that followed Victor Raul Haya De la Torre, a charismatic student and founder of the American Revolutionary Popular Alliance, better known as APRA, had put up an heroic resistance to the government forces that were trying to retake control of the city; some of the rebels, taking up positions around the city were prepared to fend off the government forces that had been sent by land, sea and air to snuff out the insurrection. They swore to fight to the end and the family heard that the carnage had been fierce and that the persecution continued.

The arrival of radio to Chorobal was an event of such magnitude that it forever changed the life of the Del Mar family, and also brought new problems for Fernando; it was nearly impossible to detach the children from this magical apparatus so that they would do their homework.

Another revolutionary invention appeared. This time on the roads: the automobile. When the first Ford model T cars arrived in the city and the proud owners took them out for a drive, they were followed by crowds of children running along beside the cars trying to jump up onto the running boards and bumpers, with the lucky ones managing to hang on for dear life for a short while. The first small trucks would appear later; they were limited to driving around the city and to the few nearby places made accessible by dangerous roads. Some drivers would later become more adventurous by venturing further and further inland, thus breaking the isolation between cities.

At the close of the 1930s Fernando realised that something was going wrong. His father was spending more time in Trujillo than at the farm and had commented that the court case had become extremely complicated. He would later find out that the unscrupulous city lawyer, through an illegal fabrication engineered by the corrupt local notary public, has double crossed him taking advantage of Don Miguel's trust, and now, incredibly, it was he, his lawyer, who was the beneficiary of the farm.

The brutal and humiliating eviction from their beloved Chorobal at the end of the 1940s, after nearly a decade of fighting in the courts, traumatised and marked the Del Mar family forever, particularly Don Miguel, who died a few years later of sorrow. It was too much for a man who had always trusted people's words more than any document. "I don't sign contracts. What for?" he would say "If I make a deal with a gentleman his word is enough, because I know that he will comply. If I sign a contract with a crook it would make no difference as he would not keep his word anyway, so why sign?"

A few years earlier, with the court case seeming to go on for ever, Fernando, realising that his younger brothers were reaching manhood, decided to speak with his father:

"Sir, I wish to speak with you about important matters." In that day and age the young spoke to their elders with great respect and formality: "Juan and Alejandro are old enough to take my place. I have heard about a mining site in the sierra, run by North Americans, that needs workers and the pay is good. I would like you to give me permission to travel and explore that possibility so that I can help you pay your debts.

Demoralised by the way that things were unravelling and knowing that he could not offer Fernando a better alternative Don Miguel replied:

"My dear son, you have helped us for so many years. You have been the main building block of this house for so long, that it would be unfair to hold you here. You will be impossible to replace and it will be even more difficult to learn to live without you. However, how can I say no to you? Go with God, son. Let Him bless you and shine on you."

The next day, with his heart in his mouth, Fernando bade farewell making sure not to cry so as not to upset his brothers. It was worse when he embraced his father before boarding the train that would take him to Trujillo. Uncontrollable tears rolled down his and Don Miguel's faces, tears of men who had gone through everything together. However, Fernando could never have imagined that he still had not experienced all the strange and adverse surprises that his destiny held in store for him.

The truck that took passengers to the Samne mining site

jostled the passengers travelling on top of the cargo without mercy. They held onto the sides of the truck for dear life and after a dusty, three hour ride they finally stopped to have lunch. While disembarking, it was difficult to make out the features of the other travellers because they were so covered in dust and dirt. "Like mill mice", smiled Fernando.

By mid-afternoon, after never ending curves and inclines, they arrived at Samne. Dirty, smelling foul and with a small cloth bag on his back in which he carried all of his worldly possessions, Fernando walked as if in a dream, scanning the immense view that surrounded him. "This place is so beautiful," he thought. He had never been in a place like this before and did not even think that it could exist. He had seen similar post cards and paintings, but he could not remember that they were this spectacular. Huge hills with little houses, flowers and animals were scattered around. "Like a Christmas nativity," he told himself "the world is so large and beautiful."

Fernando fell in love with Samne – a town with a bizarre name. This was due to the misspelling of "same name", mistakenly made by an over-tired secretary when his American boss was giving him instructions to use the same name of a town close by, when constructing the site to process the mineral extracted from nearby mines. He also became enamoured with his job as a carpenter's assistant and was happy there for many years. He soon fell in love with Maria Vargas, a pretty local girl with unusually pale eyes who was a member of a distinguished family of the town - if one can talk about distinction in a small village of four hundred people, made up of small farmers, herdsmen and one or two professionals.

Years later, in the 1950s, Fernando Del Mar would begin to build coaches, literally constructing them by hand. At first, he made them out of wood, each one taking him and a small team between two to three months to finish; much later he began to cover the wooden structures with steel; finally they were made completely out of metal. The production time improved substantially and the initial three months were reduced to one month and then finally to a week. By 1972 he had created a corporation with his sons that they called Carrocerías Del Mar S.A.; production had become an assembly line, employing about one hundred workers.

The nineteen seventies were a time of enthusiasm and industrial fervour throughout the country. It was when the Revolutionary Government of the time took the ambitious decision to turn Trujillo into a centre for automotive development for the whole Andean region; their optimistic phrase of the time was "to turn it into the Detroit of South America".

So the eighties were years of great activity and development for the company; by their end, the company was producing a coach a day and its coverage was nation-wide.

'HOW THE LACKEYS OF IMPERIALISM DIE' 1990

The bright sun shone through the national flag flapping in the breeze overhead and cast a tracery of red and white over the delicately carved colonial balconies of Lima's cathedral. The red and white shadows moved in and out of the baroque folds of the carved stone as if restlessly searching for a home.

At a nearby café, Paola and her college friends were in deep discussion about the dangerous times Peru was undergoing. None of them paid the slightest attention to the next table where a group of men were sitting, a group who were clearly important from the heavily armed body guards standing around them. If Paola and her friends had been looking, they would have seen a waiter making his way toward the men, his tray of food covered with a linen tablecloth and carried characteristically at the shoulder height demanded at a prestigious café on Lima's main square. They would not have had time to realize it was laden with a powerful charge of plastic explosives that detonated the instant he placed the tray on the table, shattering their conversation with a mighty explosion; dismembered bodies were sent flying through the air.

This was supposed to have been a clean, surgical operation against the National Director of Investigation and two of his most senior advisers, in retaliation for a recent blow dealt to one of the cells of the infamous Sendero

Luminoso movement, the Shining Path. Their intended victims were killed. But Paola and her friends were also savagely thrown from their seats and into a cement wall, leaving her friends dead and Paola paralysed from the neck down.

Among the mayhem and blood-spattered debris, somebody had been cold blooded enough to leave a red flag with the hammer and sickle; the message on it was: "This is how the lackeys of imperialism die."

In Trujillo, three hundred miles to the north of Lima, a Mercedes Benz 500 came to a stop in front of the huge metallic exit doors of a large factory. At the wheel was Don Fernando Del Mar, whom the Security guards recognized as the founder and main shareholder of the company. The doors quickly swung open and the automobile drove out onto the Pan-American Highway.

Don Fernando was apprehensive. He was driving himself to the hospital for a second gall bladder operation. Just three days beforehand he had been for a routine operation that had gone wrong; the doctor had told him that they needed to do more work. Now he was returning. It was characteristic of the man that he should drive himself.

Fernando Del Mar Saldaña was a wealthy, self made man. The owner of a few flourishing industries built up from absolutely nothing, he was a humble and nice fellow with simple but gentle manners. He sported a small moustache and an easy smile. Don Fernando had defined Spanish features with some remote traces of native blood and characteristic peaceful eyes in a relaxed face with an ample forehead. All this was packed into an unassuming muscular body.

He was, no doubt, an unpretentious man without a drop of arrogance, the undeniable consequence of his humble origins. He, like everybody else, had suffered some ups and downs in a long and difficult life, but he looked splendid for his seventy eight years of age.

The previous evening, his children and their families had gathered for a dinner at his home. His children were also partners in his companies, particularly his main concern, Carrocerías Del Mar S.A.

They had all felt a natural apprehension at their father's illness. Unusually – and perhaps prompted by the thought of his imminent operation – Don Fernando had made a speech.

He had told them that long gone were the difficult years when he had paid for his siblings' education, while at the same time raising his own children; long gone were the years of poverty and misery brought by the abusive ousting of his family from their farm. Now he needed nothing else in the world. He had avenged his childhood.

As he drove to the hospital, it was an overcast winter's day. Only foreigners thought that it was always sunny near the equator. He played Mozart on the car stereo as he watched the swooping kites pick at the detritus that lined the Pan-American Highway.

On the operating table, Don Fernando almost immediately developed a blood-clot and fell into a coma. Shortly afterwards, his condition was declared irreversible by his doctors and they advised the family that he was not expected to live for much longer. As a consequence of this, his shares and properties were distributed according to the law. After some transferring of shares within the family, control of his companies passed to his son Alvaro, who followed his father's business philosophy in which the oldest and most faithful employees became share holders, based on the Inca custom of sharing, or *ayni*.

After nearly two years in a coma, what the doctors considered a miracle occurred: Don Fernando showed signs of recuperation and began to react as though he were waking from a very long dream. In a few days he was lucid and recognised his wife and family members, although he felt extremely weak.

His wife Dona Maria reacted to his recuperation with the same serenity and fortitude with which she had reacted to his illness. She spent long hours conversing together with Don Fernando; the old man wanted to update himself on everything that had happened in the shortest time possible, not only to his friends and family but to the world. Curiously, he gave the impression of being aware of some things already, perhaps due to Dona Maria's stubbornness; she had not allowed herself to consider him unconscious and had kept telling him everything during the long hours that she had spent alone at his bedside.

Thus he already knew about Paola's terrible injuries after the bomb blast. Paola's father was one of his closest friends. Don Fernando adored her sharp wit and now they had intense discussions when she visited in her wheelchair. In spite of the cruel limitations of her paralysis, she managed to speak with a voice activated computer.

TIMES OF TERROR

Don Manuel Hurtado de Mendoza, Don Fernando's brother-in-law, was a retired school teacher and as such he had spent his life teaching and living in small inland towns and extremely poor areas of the country. As a consequence, his family of eight children and wife were permanently and directly exposed to poverty. Although his economic situation was better than Don Fernando's at the beginning of his career in the 1940s, when teachers were well-paid, by the early eighties their situation was completely reversed. But in spite of this, the affection and respect that they felt for one another was as strong as ever.

Roberto, Don Manuel's eldest son, decided to follow in his father's footsteps. He became a secondary school teacher and a university lecturer specialising in History and Geography and was a happy and extroverted young man. From an early age, like all intelligent people who are exposed to poverty, he developed a great social conscience and rebelliousness against injustice.

Roberto was a reader of serious literature, he was also an admirer of the popular tales of a romantic and legendary folk hero named Juan Pardo; a kind of Peruvian Robin Hood from the beginning of the XX century, he was a bandolier on horseback sporting a hat and a poncho who operated in the Northern Sierra where he devoted his life, and the life of his gang, to robbing the rich to distribute the wealth among the poor.

When he started to teach at the beginning of the seventies, teachers' salaries began to decrease even further. As a result, he never enjoyed a comfortable life or economic independence: just the opposite, as his situation grew worse every year. Inflation ate away at the economy, particularly affecting professors like him who lived in Lima, where the cost of living was much higher than the rest of the country. As a consequence, Roberto's and his family's life became more depressing and bleak, and later it became impossible for them to make the pay cheques last until the end of the month.

Sadly, they then borrowed money from loan sharks at exorbitant interest rates, and Roberto began to work another night shift. In the beginning this was a solution, but after some years there seemed to be no end in sight; Roberto's happy personality turned sour and he became mournful and pessimistic.

Roberto had two children: Carla, an attractive sixteen year old girl and Juan Carlos, his fourteen year old son, both intelligent and educated. During the holidays they worked in a cheap restaurant where the drunk and vulgar clientele incessantly made sexual innuendoes at Carla, who nervously and politely kept a safe distance from them.

One day, Juan Carlos could no longer hold back his anger and got into a fight with a much stronger customer, who was so drunk that Carlos seemed to get the better of him at first. But then the fight took a turn for the worse, a knife was brandished and Juan Carlos slumped to the floor clutching his stomach. Carla screamed, dropping to her knees beside her brother who, pale as a sheet, tried to remove the weapon; with the effort he lost consciousness and was rushed to the hospital's emergency unit where he was treated for serious injuries. The experience left his sister Carla traumatised.

Like a madman, their father, Roberto, walked the streets for days searching for the culprit but to no avail. Something inside him snapped and his attitude changed even further; that human beast that lives in all men awakened and demanded vengeance. He now wanted revenge for everything: for his son who was fighting for his life, for his own life that had turned out so badly and for the prevailing unfair system that had forced his children to work at such a young age and in such bad conditions. Juan Carlos survived his wounds, but lost a precious year of school.

By the late eighties, the family's life was extremely difficult. Despite working day and night, they only managed to take home miserable incomes. Roberto's wife fell ill and stopped working for months, forcing them to sell their apartment in Lima and to move to Trujillo, where they rented a small house. By now they rather used part of their family name, preferring to be called Hurtado, instead of Hurtado de Mendoza, in order to detach any connotation to a former splendour.

Roberto did not sleep well and had frequent nightmares in which he saw no future and imagined his son as a drug trafficker and his daughter as a cabaret girl or worse. He had reached the end of his tether and could not even take the holidays owed to him that he had accumulated at the college over the years. It was under these difficult circumstances that he began to attend 'democratic debates' that were nothing more than political meetings held clandestinely near the university by the "Shining Path" group. Here he ran into many of his students and some of the professors.

The disillusioned teacher had always read everything about politics but, due to his modest situation, had a predilection for leftist literature and was captivated by the insolent way and the ferocity that leftist publications used to defend the rights of the people. At the beginning he attended the meetings with trepidation but soon became accustomed to his surroundings.

The lectures that Roberto went to were given by well prepared people and made sense. Their premises were straightforward:

"Capitalism is based on the exploitation of the poor majority by a privileged minority, a minority that not only controls the means of production but the means of information as well. This is obvious and one has to be blind or stupid not to realise it. This country, a satellite of this system like the rest of the Third World, does not enjoy the advantages of capitalism. It is the place where opulent wealth and extreme poverty live together, where there is a minority with an exquisite education among a sea of ignorance and mediocrity. Where a camouflaged racism flourishes and where all the doors have closed for honest and hard working people. Instead of progress there is regression.

"Our society and our country are rotten to the core, and there will be no cure until we erase everything, until we annihilate all of the exploiters and leeches that bleed us poor people dry.

"Working brothers, this is a war that we are winning. Our cause needs no money. It needs blood.

"Many times the tree of peace, tranquillity and progress must be watered with blood and that is what we are doing, we are generously watering our beloved country with the blood of our heroes..."

Roberto rose, trembling; stirred by the speeches he had heard and with unsure steps he tiptoed to the exit that led to a dark alley. The teenage girl who was guarding the door saw that he wanted to leave and stuck her head out into the street. She looked around to see if the coast is clear and then signalled for him to leave.

That night, Roberto could not sleep until way past midnight. He could not stop thinking. He had always sympathised with the left for a simple reason: because it was in favour of the majority, the poor. The Comrade had said nothing new but Roberto now saw everything clearer;

everything fitted into place. The situation, far from improving, was worsening. Every day it was harder if not impossible to go on living. It was even harder to remain honest.

"Only the shrewd and ruthless arseholes don't suffer. They are always all right," he told himself. "Like that moneylender son of a bitch who steals my wages".

The next day was like all others, waking up at six in the morning to help Alicia make breakfast and prepare lunch boxes, working all day only to return exhausted about eleven at night.

Roberto was at a vulnerable moment in his life as a consequence of the strong depression into which he had fallen. He attended the 'democratic debates' once or twice a week, at first with a mixture of apprehension and fear, and then with more confidence. He now collaborated with the revolutionary cause by writing articles for the subversive movement's mouthpiece, under a pseudonym. However, his most effective contribution was through his lectures and his teaching desk at the National University, where he infiltrated revolutionary messages into his classes.

One day in 1988, on the sixth of June to be exact - a date that the Hurtado family would never forget as long as they lived - the devastating news arrived at their home. A pale Juan Carlos burst in, his face contorted and only just managing to stammer:

"Mother..., they have killed her. They have killed her, mother.... They have killed our Carla."

He collapsed onto the couch crying inconsolably and pointing to the television. Alicia, in total shock was only just able to turn it on, find the news channel and watch in anguish. Sure enough, a news flash reported the clash that had just occurred in Lima between the police force and a 'Shining Path' murder squad.

"Seditious elements have ambushed the Minister of Interior, General Raul Rodriguez Lara, in his automobile as he was driven from his residence to the Military Headquarters office. The attack occurred at seven forty-six this morning, at the fifth block of Primavera Avenue. When the automobile had slowed down to cross this artery to continue onto La Floresta Avenue, subversive elements detonated by remote control a large load of explosives that had been previously placed on a fruit vendor's tricycle and was parked on that corner. Simultaneously, an assassination cell appeared on the scene with machine guns and killed the General, his chauffeur Santos Ayllon Garcia, and his bodyguard Carlos Diaz Chavez. Another vehicle, carrying more of the General's security personnel, was running late and so by the time they arrived at the scene the rebels had fled to a white Toyota automobile that was waiting with its engine running. A furious exchange of bullets from automatic weapons shook the area. Three terrorists were riddled with bullets before they reached the moving vehicle: Juan Romero Lezama, twenty-two years old and a student from the Agrarian University; Carla Hurtado, nineteen and a student from the Cantuta University, and Felix Quispe Campos, twenty-six years of age, who was an employee and the General Secretary of the Workers Union of La Florida Textiles. The cost of this..."

This was the news flash that Alicia no longer heard. As if to remove any doubt, the images of the grotesque, mutilated bodies of the general and his people and the slain bodies of the terrorists appeared on the screen over and over again. Carla was there, the pretty girl, the pride of the Hurtado family, somewhat disfigured by the look of pain and the blood at the side of her mouth. It was her, of that there was absolutely no doubt.

The impact of the news was devastating for the family and their friends. No one had even suspected that Carla had become involved with the Shining Path guerrillas.

"Why? Dear God... Why? Why didn't you take me? What injustice, my God. Even you are unjust." Roberto not only lost his daughter, but also his soul. They had both been simultaneously killed. From that moment on he was never the same. For Don Fernando, Carla's great uncle, who attended the funeral, it was a devastating tragedy.

Carrocerías Del Mar S.A. had become a model company that had won the hearts of its people, not only for the quality of its products but because it helped the local economy through the creation of jobs and by actually paying its taxes, thus becoming one of the region's largest contributors. The company treated and rewarded its people well, also training and providing further education for those that wanted it. As a consequence, it was common to find young people whose greatest ambition was to work for Del Mar.

Its directors and executives had a clear idea of the role that modern industry should play in society, and wanted to create a strong company. "It is a shame that in poor countries there are so few strong and well-organised companies able to survive its founders. It is as if a curse existed that when the founder dies the company dies", Don Fernando often said.

The early dream of providing homes for all their workers had already been realised and they now wanted to attain another of their workers' dreams: the ownership of a car. Many had already obtained this. How was this all possible? Because of the founder's philosophy; "The more we pay our people, the more money they will have and the more they spend, or save. It is the only way that the whole society will become prosperous."

So, despite terrorism, the company continued to flourish under successive governments. The executives were aware of the world wide changes that were occurring with the public's preferences, market tendencies and the technological changes that affected and benefited them; because they often visited the largest coach manufacturing industries in the rest of the world and were visited by foreign specialists in turn. They based their updates on the certainty that theirs was a quite unique kind of industry.

In 1991, Juan Carlos, Roberto's son, was now twenty-two. He had been enrolled for more than a year in the Shining Path cell that operated from somewhere in La Libertad's huge mountain range. Only his parents knew his secret. They knew that one day Juan Carlos could no longer contain his deep hatred for a system which, according to him, had killed his sister. He had decided to give into his hunger for justice and – although he never said it - for vengeance. He had sworn to avenge his beloved Carla's death, so tragically killed in the prime of her life.

Juan Carlos had quite a complex personality. He was a dreamer and easily influenced young man with a resentful character, quite uneasy among his piers in spite of his rather handsome features. He was not an intellectual, nor a well informed person, but was rather impulsive with a small degree of an inferiority complex.

His parents could not deter him, although truth be told, Roberto did not try too hard. He seemed to endorse his decision with silence; he himself was no longer physically fit for military operations.

"May God be with you my son. Carry your mother's and my blessing with you and if I can serve the cause somehow, let me know."

In this way a new member swelled the ranks of a movement which was 'guerrilla' to some and 'terrorist' to others,. "It is easy to preach about the popular war but how heartrending it is to live it firsthand", thought Roberto.

Father and son walked alone that warm summer night, absorbed in their own thoughts. They headed to the *España* square where Juan Carlos would board the '*Transportes Otuzco*' night bus. Roberto, who has not done so for a long time, put his arm around his son's shoulders. He wanted to touch him, feel him perhaps for the last time. He could feel the tension in his son's young and athletic body. At the same time, Juan Carlos placed his arm around his father's waist and they walked the last block to the square in complete silence.

The time to say goodbye arrived a little before they reached the ticket office. They wanted to avoid being seen together as Juan Carlos was travelling with false documents and under a new name.

"We are going to eradicate them, father. We are going to destroy this miserable system and rewrite history."

"It will be so, son. God has demanded it."

A kiss on the cheek and a long embrace sealed the separation; the boy, walking a few steps forward, was soon lost amongst the rest of the travellers.

Roberto felt like dying. This was the second or third time that he had experienced this horrible feeling. The thought of running after his son and stopping him crossed his mind for a fraction of a second but it was only that: a fleeting idea that passed briefly through his imagination, a thought about which he would later feel ashamed.

However, as a history and geography teacher he could not stop thinking about what his son had told him about re-writing history until he remembered the American Ambrose Bierce, who had described history as "an account, mostly false, of events unimportant, which are brought about by rulers, mostly knaves, and soldiers, mostly fools".

CONFUSION. 1992

The 12th of March was the day when the entire Del Mar family, their close relatives and friends took a break from their duties and gathered to celebrate Dona Maria's birthday. On this occasion in 1992 they would celebrate her eightieth birthday; therefore the programme that her children had prepared included a full orchestra and fireworks. Time was when Roberto, the professor, had always participated in these events with his guitar; however in the past few years he had, understandably, become a bit of a hermit.

Weeks earlier Don Fernando had invited Roberto and his wife to spend the weekend at his farm to discuss the possibility of their attending the birthday party. By chance, Alvaro, Don Fernando's son, also showed up.

"Uncle, you know how much I love Aunt Maria and you," said Roberto, "and nothing would make me happier than to accept the invitation. But the truth is, I don't want to ruin your party. With Alicia ill and Juan Carlos so far away in Europe on that scholarship," he lied, "I am not in the mood for anything."

"We all have our problems, cousin", said Alvaro as he handed him a glass of beer, "but we don't let them get the better of us."

The simple and fresh atmosphere, in spite of the gruelling heat, was typical of orchards in northern Peru. There were mango trees, avocado trees and banana plants interspersed throughout the property and the ever-present passion-fruit vines under which they sat on a paved patio. Don Fernando wore his wide-brim straw hat, a white shirt and trousers, and sat back, barefoot, in his rocking chair. With his skin toasted by the sun and his white moustache, he looked like a man from another time.

"What do you think about the current political situation, Roberto? Fujimori is approaching his third year in power. Do you think that he is what the country needs?" inquired the old man after some initial conversation.

President Fujimori had been the surprise winner of the previous election. Of Japanese descent, his strong-arm approach to terrorism went hand-in-hand with a 'man-of–the–people' image; he had ridden around in a tractor to make his election speeches, and had made much of not being from one of the established parties.

"To be honest uncle, I must confess that I am confused," replied Roberto. "You know my political tendencies. I think that this time the people made a good decision when they elected such a 'famously unknown' individual; only a few can deny his audacity and pragmatism. However, I think he is wrong to have such a brutal anti-subversive strategy, where he is committing excesses beyond words. We'll have to wait a bit longer before I can give you a proper answer."

"Indeed, I know your ideology and respect it", replied Don Fernando while he filled his glass. "I also admire your honesty when you contradict the official position of the so called 'Left'. What do you think, Alvaro?"

"As a business man, I would have liked to see Vargas Llosa win the election, although I am not so sure anymore. He was, involuntarily perhaps, filling his future government with political dinosaurs who wouldn't have allowed him to change anything. Now, even though I personally like much of what the new president is doing, I'm confused as well."

Don Fernando adjudicated: "We all are and will be

confused for some time. Events in the world and our country are developing and will continue developing at such a breakneck speed that whoever says they aren't confused is a liar or an uninformed boaster."

"Who could have known several years ago that we would see the sudden disappearance of the Soviet Union?" asked Don Fernando. "The end of communism, that was like saying today that in one or two years capitalism will disappear. It was the other way around then, people declared that communism would bury capitalism and all or most of us believed it. One had to be blind to miss the unstoppable advancement that it made all over the world"

"Now that Capitalism alone survives, now that all of the means of production and communications are in their hands with no counterweight to balance it… Do you really think that there is hope for the poor? Roberto asked avidly. "One should think that a counter force is necessary, a balance of power. One should not forget that even the devil is an element for stability in religions…."

Juan Carlos belonged to a guerrilla column that was being trained somewhere in the mountains near the Amazon jungle; it was an idyllic place with a tropical climate and luxurious vegetation, seemingly at odds with the rigours of military training.

The people he lived with were his own age and one could see in their faces the rich mix of races – Spanish, African, Japanese, Chinese as well as native ones – that had gone into forming Peru. They were very disparate people: some were soulless people who only desired vengeance; others were romantics and committed to the cause like Juan Carlos. Nevertheless the great majority of rebels were marginal, desperate and intransigent individuals who had entered the movement because they simply didn't have anything else to do in life.

They had to undergo exhausting military training in sabotage and defence but like all people their age, especially when in a mixed group of men and women, they tried to live as intensely as they could, conscious that each day could be their last.

Although Juan Carlos was one of the calmest and most serious members in the detachment, he was not averse to the continuous promiscuity and abundance of temptation. He felt a great attraction for Ivonne, a good-looking local girl with few moral scruples. One day, while they were resting in the jungle, she said jokingly to him:

"Rodrigo," addressing him by his combat name, "Carmen says that she wants to sleep with you."

Carmen was sitting beside them and reacted to this with a coy smile.

Juan Carlos replied with out thinking, "Maybe, Ivonne my *chiquita*, but you know that you're the one I fancy."

Ivonne continued flirtatiously, "Why not make do with both of us?"

The three of them slipped down to the riverbank, giggling as they went and stripping off their combat clothes.

After Don Fernando had slept for a bit in his hammock and while the rest of the family was in the swimming pool, the conversation with Roberto and Alvaro resumed.

"Injustice, corruption and poverty, and one could add ignorance and racism are all children of the same mother" said Roberto, "the mother Capitalism, where the minority wins and the majority loses."

Don Fernando moved to his rocking chair again and stretched his legs, crossing his bare feet on a footstool; he rested his chin on his hands and looked into the distance saying:

"Capitalism is a deified and cursed word; passionately loved and bitterly hated. And what is it finally, other than the name of a human creation with all of its virtues and all of its defects as with everything that man makes or invents?

Without passion it is nothing more than an economic system that, until now, has shown that it is the only system that creates massive wealth; wealth that may or may not be spread fairly and equally among the people. To me, capitalism does not do the spreading well, if left to its own devices, hence the injustice you refer to. Consequently, it is the distribution of wealth that needs to be looked at."

"To think that capitalism is an immutable and already perfect system per se, is a huge mistake", he said. "It is an error in thinking that capitalism alone is bad or that the one that is practised in North America, Europe, Japan, the Scandinavian countries and the rest of the world is one and the same. Nothing could be further from the truth. Capitalism is a living organism that is susceptible to evolution and is developing as such."

Don Fernando slowly shifted position in his rocking chair. He realised that he had his small audience's complete attention and continued:

"Communism is another human creation, loved and equally vilified; beautiful in theory but fatal in practice. What is fairer than us all having the same opportunities in life, where there are no poor or rich, and no misery or injustice. Everything seemed to indicate that communism was the society of the future. Who with a clear mind and a good heart could disdain that ideal society, that paradise on earth?"

"This is how it advanced and deeply pierced the intellectual spheres of the world" he continued. "The young fervently embraced it. To be an avant-garde intellectual was synonymous to being a socialist or a communist. Whoever was not was considered a reactionary. Then maturity set in and the precept that says: "If you are under thirty and you are not a communist you have no heart, but if you are over thirty and you are still a communist you have no brain", came into force."

"The rest of communism is history," said Don Fernando, "what we really need now, is someone who can explain to me why, in this country, at the twilight of the twentieth century, a group of soulless people – although I don't doubt that some have good intentions - still haven't heard that communism has died. Or perhaps worse, they may have already found out but they don't give a damn; and continue with their sermons and actions out of revenge or for 'political validity' To assume for oneself the representation of the poor of a country, to want to impose an expired ideology by force, is barbaric arrogance in its most miserable expression."

"Years ago" remembered Don Fernando, "a Spanish friend of mine who was a member of Felipe Gonzalez's first government, said to me: 'I do not understand your Shining Path's manifesto for it seems like a retrograde sermon dating from the Stone Age. It is a sad curiosity that is discussed at meetings of European Socialist intellectuals with some ridicule. Even the name, when I first heard it, seemed ridiculous for a political organisation.' I explained that the population had repudiated the Shining Path at the polls and explained that the complete name was 'The Peruvian Communist Party for Jose Carlos Mariategui's Shining Path'. 'How indigestible!' he said."

Don Fernando had realised that Roberto was becoming uncomfortable with the mention of the Shining Path. As he didn't want to hurt him - he was too fond of him for that - he tempered his criticism, and assuming a more reflective attitude, as if thinking out loud, continued:

"Making a strong intellectual effort I can try to put myself in their shoes and understand their reasons and their anger. But to blow up bridges and high tension towers that leave hospitals, schools and work centres with no power, where their own family members are educated, work or are attended, can only be barely justified once, or maybe twice; but to continue to do this for twelve long years. To terrorise and kill innocent people has no justification here or in the China of the communist revolution, which seems to be their role model."

"Let's make a mental effort" challenged Don Fernando, "and let's believe that the Shining Path is, as they say, winning. Now let's ask: Winning what? Winning the will of the people or their hate?"

"Speaking of violence and arms", interrupted Alvaro, addressing his father, "do you find it moral and ethical that at the end of the century, weapons of mass destruction - strategic weapons as they are called- are still produced, investing billions of dollars when the majority of the world lives in a precarious situation?"

"No, I could never find a justification for that aberration" answered the old man, who now walked back and forth with his arms behind his back. "How can it be moral or ethical? What happens with the arms industry is that it is a business like any other, and it can not cease to exist all of a sudden. The economy, particularly the economy of some countries, are so dependent, addicted I would say, to this industry that if it suddenly disappears it would be something like a heart attack; gigantic companies would collapse, creating unemployment and an economic recession with unpredictable consequences. The dynamics of this industry can not be stopped suddenly by pulling a lever or pressing a button, the same way that one can not suddenly stop the propeller of a turbine when electricity is cut."

"I think that the same thing is happening in our country with the revolutionary movement or whatever we want to call it. A man who has never been to Peru and possibly hasn't the least interest in its existence, has already pressed the button and cut off the fuel that fed the Shining Path some time ago. I am talking about Mikhail Gorbachev. And the fuel was not the economic or logistic aid that he did or didn't provide, but the philosophical-political basis; the mysticism that created the faith to begin projects that would have otherwise been abandoned by reason or common sense. Thus, the revolutionary movement cannot suddenly stop because its dynamics, its inertia fed by the desire for revenge, makes it continue" pointed out Don Fernando.

Suddenly, the light bulbs flickered. Because of the distance and the direction of the wind, the small group had not felt an enormous explosion that had blown the Trujillo electrical station into oblivion. Roberto and Alicia had no idea that their son - their only son - hardly ten kilometres away from them, was receiving his baptism by fire.

At that precise moment, Juan Carlos was running for his life in the middle of a hell of gun powder, dust and fire. Suffocating and with madness in his eyes he ran, limping, towards Comrade Alberto, who had been mortally wounded by guards before they were immolated in a gigantic fire ball.

He desperately tried with his dirty hands to stop the haemorrhage that was flowing from the huge gash in the boy's chest. The infernal roar of the explosion, the hot blood on his hands and the pale and imploring face of his friend made a terrible impact on Juan Carlos who now acted like a zombie. Instinctively, he eased Alberto onto his shoulders and carried him, staggering in a zigzag pattern to safety.

"Where was it that they would pick us up?" All that he could remember was nervously activating the detonator of the dynamite loaded on the truck, while Alberto placed a heavy anvil on the vehicle's accelerator before sending it on its way to its target. He could not get his bearings due to the smoke, to say nothing of the panic that had gripped him. The lights of an approaching vehicle through the cloud of dust brought him back to reality.

With his heavy load and with great difficulty he approached the four wheel drive vehicle where two strongly armed comrades opened the door. They took one look at Alberto, exchanged glances and left the lifeless body strewn on the sand. Juan Carlos, still in a state of shock, wanted to object but he was suddenly thrust backwards against the seat by the abrupt acceleration of the vehicle. He slowly lost consciousness while staring at the modern weapons his companions carried.

"The weapons industry" continued Don Fernando "is one of the greatest businesses in the world. It consumes more resources than those invested in health and education together" But of course, as it is a great business, six hundred billion dollars in arms have been exported during the last twenty years; the ex-USSR, the United States of America and the UK being the greatest exporters. Ideology aside, business is business."

Roberto listened intensely to the old man who continued speaking with a calm voice -a mixture of university professorship and religious sermon- without showing fatigue. His initial discomfort had disappeared and now it was even possible to admit that he enjoyed and felt at ease; perhaps because the criticisms and self-criticisms were sincere. Now it is he, Roberto, who paced slowly back and forth.

"Uncle, going back to the subject of our country, you apparently seem happy with the present social situation, that you don't really care that thousands of children die every day because they are undernourished or because of a lack of medical aid; or that new generations will not find the smallest opportunity to progress and escape the vicious circle in which they are trapped, while the politicians, military and corrupt magistrates run the country at their whim and for their own benefit."

"No nephew, it is not like that. If I have given you that impression I apologise" pronounced the old man. "I thought that we were all starting from the premise that this is a sick country with many limitations. That I have not named them does not mean that I accept them, or that I like them."

"I am against everything that involves fetishes and archaic dogma, but nothing else. There is much to preserve in this country, although many people don't think so. If that makes me conservative, then I am conservative. What I really think is that I am an old man who matured the wrong way around, the opposite to apples: that are first green, then

145

pink and finally red. First I was red, then pink and now green; very green. No. Not for the reason that you are thinking," he joked – he well knew that in Spanish *Viejo verde,* a green old man, means 'a dirty old man'. There was a burst of laughter from the others and a call from Dona Maria to remind them that the meal was served.

After dinner and under the light of the moon, Don Fernando and the two men sat and drank coffee around a small table on the patio.

"So father, now tell us how you think that our country can escape from the mess it's in", Alvaro asked adding with a smile: "Who should be killed?"

Don Fernando reclined his rocking chair completely, and took a sip of his coffee before answering.

"Aside from the most important thing, which is to be able to impose the Rule of Law and then get rid of ignorance, we have to control the stupid discrimination and racism that dominates our lives."

"Think of the Inca civilisation. Anyone in the world who has some education has heard of it. They speak of it with respect and admiration as its culture was attained in complete isolation. Let's continue with the Spanish culture and race, but leave aside the question of whether those who came to America were the best or the worst of Spain, which to me is nothing more than a pointless argument. Those who say that the worst came, demonstrate a crass ignorance of history as they forget that Australia was populated with convicts from British jails and Australians today are proud of that heritage."

"Spain was a world power for centuries and is on its way to being so again", the old man pointed out. "The bravery and courage of Spain's children are legendary and nobody doubts their wisdom and artistic sensitivity. Right now it is one of the ten strongest economies on the planet. Therefore gentlemen, we come from a combination of two splendid races. You may argue that as such, we are a mixture, but I ask you, what country isn't?"

As always, the terrorists had two or three well planned alternative escape routes, depending on last-minute circumstances.

The attack had been perpetrated at exactly seven thirty-four and they had been speeding north along their chosen escape route for the past twenty-five minutes. Juan Carlos had recuperated, changed out of his blood-stained shirt, and, like his companions, had his weapon at the ready.

They were lucky and passed the check point of Chicama without incident; now they were approaching the town of Casagrande, listening with excited attention as the radio transmitted news of their attack. They learned that the police had set up substantial road blocks at all of the routes out of the city, while the army was concentrating on the northern routes.

Comrade Alfonso, in charge of the operation, did not want to take unnecessary risks by passing through Casagrande as they had originally planned. Instead they left the Pan American highway and headed west towards the beach at Paijan, where they abandoned the vehicle in a pre-arranged spot. At a nearby farm a female comrade was waiting for them with a pick-up truck and clean clothes.

They washed, changed and left the weapons with the girl, then headed towards the port of Chicama. It was the early hours of a black night and at a street corner, under a lamppost, they saw a small group of foreign-looking youngsters carrying surf boards and signalling that they wanted a lift. 'Perfect camouflage' thought Alfonso who was at the wheel and pulled over for them. They were two Australians, a New Zealander and a Peruvian who were heading to the beach where they planned to spend a few days surfing.

Chicama Port was a remote beach on the northern coast of Peru, famous worldwide among surfers as it had, apparently, the longest waves in the world. As a consequence, young tourists continued to defy the serious warnings issued by their embassies not to visit Peru because of terrorism. To better camouflage themselves, two of the rebels got out of the driving cabin and travelled on the flatbed of the truck, sitting on the floor with the foreigners.

PART IV

INTO THE LION'S DEN

Roberto was unable to sleep for nights after listening to Don Fernando. He couldn't stop thinking about his daughter and it tormented him to think that his beloved Carla might have died for no reason. And at any moment someone might bring him the news that his son, his last hope and reason for living, had also been killed, and for what? This worry hammered away at his brain and almost overwhelmed him. During those nightmarish nights he became obsessed with the idea of recovering his son no matter what it took; he punished himself by thinking that his anxiety was cowardly, not revolutionary, and he continued his daily life tormented by misgivings.

In the early evening of Saturday, 12th of September, 1992 the country was shaken with the news that would soon reach the entire world. Abimael Guzman, the supreme leader and founder of the Shining Path, had been captured by the Peruvian police along with a considerable number of other ringleaders.

On Sunday 13th, Roberto was on the brink of despair and madness. He had spent all night glued to the radio and television, anxiously waiting for the frequent news flashes. He needed to know who else had been caught, as he wanted to make sure that his son was not among them. Exuding a calmness that he did not have, he tried to console his wife, who was also heartbroken and who had spent the night praying.

Roberto devoured almost all of the morning papers before changing to go to church with Alicia, as was their custom every Sunday. They spent the rest of the day nervously watching television and with the radio turned on in the background, as there had been an announcement that President Fujimori would formally announce the capture at eight o'clock on all channels.

At eight o'clock there was still no news. The President appeared three hours later and the tension in the Hurtado home increased to unbearable limits. The message confirmed what they already knew but with more details, and did not mention additional names to those that had been mentioned earlier. The famous Doctor Guzman or 'President Gonzalo' appeared sometimes depressed, sometimes defiant, with an enigmatic and sinister look in his eyes that made him resemble a caged beast.

Roberto found it hard to sleep that night and managed only a short doze, waking drenched in sweat and trembling in his distress. He consoled himself with the knowledge that the heist had been in Lima, as he was sure that his son was still in the mountains of La Libertad. At day break, he could stand it no longer and decided to go and see his uncle Fernando, so that he could confess everything once and for all, and ask his advice.

"We must bring him back", was the old man's immediate and conclusive reply. "There is no other solution" He asked no other questions and did not seem surprised by his nephew's confession.

Speaking in the plural, he clearly included himself in this quest:

"We must organise the rescue immediately, there is no time to lose."

"And what happens if he doesn't want to come back?"

"Leave that to me, I'll take care of that," insisted Don Fernando.

"I'll take care of that?" pondered Roberto, worried: 'What does the old man have in mind?'

Don Fernando calmly explained what he planned to do. He knew where the guerrillas operated and that their headquarters had to be in the north; far into the mountain range of La Libertad, near the Marañón River. It would take them four days to get there: two days by road and two on horseback; he knew the route because he had travelled that area around sixty years ago, pointing out that "as we are in Peru, it probably hasn't changed much".

Roberto was willing to do anything, to take any risk; he didn't care about the dangers involved and was willing to give up his life for his son.

It was still early and they were alone. Maria and her maid were working with the television on in another room and could not hear them. Roberto still couldn't believe that Don Fernando had clearly included himself in the operation.

"You and I will go; no-one else must know about this, I repeat, no-one; not even our wives."

"But I can do it alone, uncle."

"No nephew, you can't do it alone, and I will tell you why: because you do not know the area and because a person travelling alone at your age would be highly suspicious. The rebels or the police will kill you without hesitation if they don't get a coherent answer to the question of why you are there. And if they don't kill you, drug dealers will do so thinking that you are from the secret police or another faction that wants to compete with them. That area is infested with trigger happy criminals. An old man like me will not arouse suspicion. You can say that you are a cattle dealer looking for a new route to transport your animals to the coast - and I am your terminally ill uncle, a crazy old man who is returning to his homeland to spend his last days in peace. Who will doubt an eighty year old man?"

"But uncle, this is crazy. You don't have any reason to

expose yourself to danger; it is not your problem. I can't allow it."

"The one who will not allow you to speak to him like this is me. Calm down. A young life, whoever it is, is valuable to me and to our country; even more so if we are talking about a misguided young man who happens to be the son of a beloved relative."

Don Fernando was conscious of the risks that he would be running by penetrating a red zone. He was very aware that they would be entering the lion's den and that nothing would make the rebels happier than the capture of a rich old man so that they could then demand a high ransom for him. Or even worse, now that they were desperate, they could exchange him along with other important kidnap victims for no less than Abimael Guzman.

"I know this very well, and that is precisely why nobody else must know about it. Do you understand? ¡Absolutely nobody! Any indiscretion, and your son's and our lives will be worthless. We can't run that risk."

They worked out a plan: in a few days time they would go to Punta Sal on the northern coast of Peru 'to go fishing' for a week. They had chosen the place as it was remote and had no telephone.

"You know Maria, Roberto has been stressed for a long time and needs to rest, chat, find himself, and I can help with that as he really trusts me. Furthermore, I myself need a bit of sun and tranquillity. You can take advantage of this time to visit your grandchildren in Lima. If we are enjoying ourselves, we might stay a few more days. They tell us that the place is very popular and that there may be no rooms; if so, we'll stay at Cabo Blanco or Caleta de la Cruz."

So as not to rouse anyone's suspicions, they planned to drive a rented van from home but to leave it behind in a secure garage on the outskirts of Trujillo. This was because it was not a good idea to drive into the mountains in a new vehicle, as it would call attention to themselves. They would leave the light clothes for their trip to the north in the vehicle and they would buy warm clothes, ponchos and hats for the mountains; if they were second-hand, all the better. Neither would they carry much money as it would be suspicious. The other details would be developed along the way according to the circumstances. Anyway, they had no idea of what awaited them.

They left letters for their wives in case the worst happened and they did not return. They needed to leave them with a person they trusted completely, whose loyalty and discretion has been tested and Fernando did not have to think twice about who it should be. He picked up the phone and asked for Mr. Enrique Morachimo. Someone explained that he was not in, that he had gone to a restaurant called 'El Mochica' in Moche with some friends. It was already mid-morning when they took the old man's car out of the garage and headed in search of Enrique.

On the way Don Fernando told Roberto a bit about Enrique Morachimo and explained that he was probably the person whom he trusted most, with the exception of his wife and one or two family members:

"He's a very nice man, a distant descendant of a famous Chimú chief. He is one of the best employees in my company and has proved his loyalty in the good times and the bad. Over twenty-five years ago, he arrived barefoot at the factory: it was not easy for us to get him into the habit of wearing shoes. I think that, after time, the nails scattered on the factory floor changed his mind. He was clearly an intelligent young man with an ability to learn and after a few months there was no machine that he could not take apart and reassemble blindfolded. He is now the head of maintenance, with several engineers working under him. But he is still the same modest and calm person that he was before; I love him dearly."

They entered the Moche restaurant. There, at a large table among several people drinking beer and listening to the music that three of the group was playing on their guitars was Enrique. He looked about fifty years old, of a stocky dark build, with a contented expression and strong physique. An old man with white hair and thin beard sat at the head of the table: this was Don Cornelio, Enrique's father.

When they approached the table everyone made room for them to join the group, an invitation they felt they couldn't decline. Don Cornelio and Don Fernando warmly embraced and the former expressed phrases full of admiration for his successful peer. They continued to drink and the musicians stood up and dedicated a few old Creole waltzes to Don Fernando and the 'guest'.

The guest was a gentleman of approximately the same age as Enrique, eccentrically dressed in a red shiny track suit with a large yellow lego, dark glasses and a camera that hung from his neck. He seemed to be ahead of the rest of the group as far as the drinking went and insisted on speaking Spanglish, as if he couldn't remember certain words in Spanish or pronounce them well – in spite of the mocking smiles and looks from his friends.

"This Moche guy has been living in the United States for over fifteen years and says that he has forgotten his Spanish", commented one of his friends, who also looked 'well pickled'. After another glass the 'gringo' became very sentimental and began to hug everybody.

"Cousin", he addressed Enrique, "you are so lucky to have a simple and peaceful life. But tomorrow I will go back to the States to work; to put my head down and do nothing else but work and work. Life away from my native land is tough, cousin; away from family and friends. Of course we have our homes, our cars and other comforts; but there is more to life brother, you know." And addressing the rest of those present, he added, "I would give any thing to have my Cousin Enrique's life."

After a while Don Fernando and Roberto stood up, apologised for the interruption, and motioned Enrique to one side. Old man Morachimo, who was nearby, overheard Don Fernando asking Enrique to accompany him for a moment. He patted his son on the back and told him "go son, go". And the three, apologising again, climbed into the car and left.

Three days later, at six twenty in the morning, Don Fernando and Roberto boarded the 'Transportes Andinos' bus that would take them to Huamachuco. What a difficult and dusty road it had been. The old man had forgotten about the extent of this punishment. Dead tired, with altitude sickness, dirty and with aching bones, they disembarked at the Plaza de Armas of Huamachuco at around four o'clock in the afternoon. It was a large, cold and deserted square, with only a few trees giving it a breath of life. They bought hot chicken broth from a street vendor near the hotel and took a walk around the city.

"Near here," explained Roberto, "Tupac Yupanqui, the Inca conqueror of this territory, sat with the great Huamachuco to agree to a treaty and arrange the assimilation of his powerful kingdom into the Inca Empire."

"And in that house," added Don Fernando, "the Liberator of America, Don Simón Bolívar, lived while preparing his troops for some of the decisive battles for independence from Spain."

Some locals told them that trucks left very early to El Pallar from the market square, which was just two blocks away. They set out at around five o'clock the next morning. Roberto was wearing a thick jacket, scarf and hat and carrying a travel case that hung over his shoulder. Don Fernando was similarly attired but wearing a brown poncho; he had his hands in his pockets to protect them from the cold. A small bag made his poncho appear bulky on his back. Roberto was much calmer now that he was doing something real to recover his son.

The truck was being loaded with cases of beer, sacks of rice, live animals and, naturally, people. It was called 'The

King of Curves'. Although this worried Don Fernando and Roberto, they could not help smiling when they saw that on the back of the vehicle was a painted and extremely curvaceous woman. They hoped that the driver was also a master of the curves of the hazardous roads.

The rattling, rutted road had innumerable bends and tiresome ascents and descents. Sitting on cases of beer, they held on tightly to the main beam that served as the base for an awning when it rained, which was frequently. It reminded Don Fernando of his first trip to the mountains and of the many others that he had taken throughout his life. He recognised places one by one and thought about how strange his life had ended up being. He compared the truck in which they travelled, to the first class compartments of transatlantic planes in which he frequently flew. He compared the little five dollars a night hotel in which they had stayed to the five star hotels of Europe and the United States that he was accustomed to.

The streets of Huamachuco were so different from the streets of London, New York and Tokyo. And yet he could not deny the indescribable charm that these trips to the interior of Peru had. As for Roberto, he was in deep thought about how he could reach his son, what awaited them and how they could convince Juan Carlos to return with them. His thoughts were interrupted when the truck stopped at Yanasara to unload and so the passengers could have lunch.

The rain ceased and the sky beyond the mountains was beautifully clear. They had forgotten the splendour of the Andean sky. With never ending ups and downs, they had not noticed that they had descended to a considerably lower altitude. They now observed this beautiful and unkempt landscape with admiration and certain distrust. They were already in the dangerous 'red zone' that the Sendero had made their own.

The truck parked in front of the 'Tupac Amaru Agrarian Production Cooperative', the new name of what was once the mighty landowner Don Pancho Pinillos's ranch. Don Fernando remembered having met this gentleman many years before when he arrived on a gorgeous chestnut horse at the nearby thermal baths. He wore a wide-brim white hat and a light brown poncho that matched the colour of his horse. He had greeted all of the bathers, including Fernando, without dismounting, conversed with one of them and left just as he had arrived, in a quiet and unassuming way.

One of the other bathers told him a little about Don Pancho Pinillos, who was about forty five years old and single. He remembered that this last piece of information had surprised him. Word had it that his properties were immense and that one needed weeks to cross them from end to end; they had been in his family since colonial times.

The *casa-hacienda*, the country house, was now run down and half occupied by offices and the co-operative president's residence, the other half rubble – a result of one of the terrorist attacks.

While the truck unloaded sugar and rice at the co-operative, most of the passengers had lunch in a run down place across the street. They all ate the same meal. From here on in the sophistication of eating with any choice at all at a restaurant did not exist; there was a set meal of one dish each day.

Don Fernando estimated that the last time that he had been there was fifty-six years ago. He must have been about twenty-four when the Northern Peru Mining Corporation, the American company where he worked, ceased operations for two or three months. This was a long time before he had met and fallen in love with Maria. He couldn't recall exactly why the company had closed for that time. Was it because the Second World War had begun? No, he couldn't remember. But the company had temporarily discharged the workers and when Fernando went in search of temporary work, he did not go to the coast as expected, but to the mountains. He wanted to get to know more of this mysterious world of never-ending peaks that had opened up to him the first time he entered it.

While they ate, an ancient radio trembled on a shelf and seemed to dance to the rhythm of the native song, a *huayno* playing at full volume. "At any moment it will fall or start to smoke and fall apart," Don Fernando commented.

"Roberto, can palm trees grow at this altitude?" inquired the old man.

"Yes, they can. We are in a low area bordered by hills that create a more moderate and temperate micro-climate. Why do you ask?" asked the geography teacher.

"Because I remember being impressed by how pretty this ranch was originally, with its brilliant white walls, red tiled roof and gorgeous tall palm trees. The house has survived more or less, although they have not repaired or repainted it for half a century. However, I don't see the palm trees or the bougainvillaea that contrasted so beautifully with the white walls over which it hung."

"One of two things could have happened: either your memory has betrayed you, or the plants have died from neglect," suggested Roberto.

"Died" thought the old man, "as in so many other ranches in Peru. They died or they were chopped down to make firewood, in the same way that the *campesinos* killed the extremely expensive livestock that had been imported for reproduction."

They had left Yanasara behind with its badly kept fields and its nonexistent livestock. Their final destination was 'El Pallar', a hamlet of just a few houses, which they thought they would arrive at before nightfall. Once there, they hoped to rent horses that would take them to Santa Elena.

The old rattle trap of a truck started up again and Roberto worried about his uncle's health. They noticed that new passengers had boarded the truck; there was one particular twenty-six or twenty-seven year old, a tall, strong man who had an elusive gaze and looked as though he was from the coast. He attracted their attention because he stayed somewhat detached from the rest, not speaking to anyone and not even getting off the truck to have lunch. They didn't mind that he did not speak as they were not interested in striking up a friendship with anyone; they thought it would be dangerous to do so. Fortunately, the noise of the truck prevented any social courtesies other than a smile or a nod as a greeting.

Roberto was nervous and tried to distract himself by mentally visualising the exact geographical location of El Pallar. But his mind returned, over and over again, to the situation in which his son had found himself. "The last time that I received a letter from Juan Carlos, it was very laconic and with no return address. He mentioned that he was working directly with the businessmen, an analogy that indicated that he was already a member of the mid-ranks of the movement."

Although the shaking of the lorry and the change in altitude and climate intensified the ache that Don Fernando had in one of his legs, he did not complain nor even mention it. His mind digressed to other things: "It was a huge mistake to carry out the Agrarian Reform the way it was done. It is interesting to see how the best intentions in the world can do so much harm to precisely those that they try to benefit. Once the dust has settled and we can see more clearly, history may call General Velasco a sincere and well-intentioned leader, but it will also be frank about the immense harm that his Socialist Revolution did to Peru. It impeded progress and its lingering effects are still felt. Far from allowing the country to advance as Velasco wanted, the result was that it regressed, falling backwards."

"After Velasco's left-wing coup in 1968, wealthy land-owners were deprived of most of their holdings and their land was re-distributed to the community and to cooperatives: three-quarters of agrarian land in Peru was put under community management. But the success of the land reforms created a dispossessed middle class, who no longer had their land to fall back on, and it was from the children of these dispossessed, particularly the university graduates, that the Sendero Luminoso had drawn some of its strength: Abimael Guzmán, the Sendero leader, had drawn many of his more intellectual cadres from students he had taught when a teacher at the University in Ayacucho, and given them a Maoist zeal for total solutions that had led to the brutal slaughter of all who disagreed with them. This had provoked a military response from the Government which some thought equally brutal."

"And here are the results" thought Don Fernando: "Where there was once some order and progress, now there is only chaos, abandonment and devastation. The General wanted to break the backbone of the landowners and there's no doubt he succeeded. What a pity that he also crippled two or three generations of Peruvians in the process. The tyranny of often despotic landlords was bad and abusive, but the cure ended up being far worse than the disease."

The awning had been set up over the back of the truck because of a downpour and so the noise of the engine was less noticeable; the drumming of the rain on the canvas and the increasingly warm temperature as they descended lulled the travellers into a deep sleep, in spite of 'The King of Curves'' eternal bouncing on its springs.

Nearly ten hours after leaving Huamachuco and after numerous stops for one reason or another - such as having to pay the "revolutionary quota for the popular war", collected by six lads armed with automatic weapons who asked everyone for identification, made routine questions and fell for the story of the cattle dealer and the crazy uncle - they arrived at El Pallar. Because his legs had gone numb, Don Fernando could no longer walk and so descended from the truck over his nephew's shoulder. Roberto had an awful premonition.

Fortunately Don Fernando's legs had just fallen asleep and, with the help of a quickly improvised cane, they advanced towards the house of one Ruperta, where they had been told they could rent horses.

"No, not anymore, now we don't rent anything", said the toothless old lady they found beside the stream; she did not even look up from the clothes she was washing on the rocks.

"This is an emergency, Señora", Roberto explained to the lady as he walked down towards her, and in a low voice added: "My uncle is hopelessly ill and is going to Marcabal to look for his sons, so he can die in peace there."

The old lady raised her eyes and squinted curiously, trying to recognise the older man who was sitting exhausted on a rock.

"And what is this man's name?" she asked.

"Fernando", answered the old man himself, "Fernando Alegria."

After a long pause, as if searching for the name in her memory, the old lady – who could have been no older that fifty-five but looked far older due to the tough life that she had led – inquired:

"Which one of them are you then?"

"Don Cornelio's son; I left the ranch when I was a boy."

"Don Cornelio? Don Cornelio? I don't remember him,' exclaimed the old lady. "But then there were so many." She seemed to change her mind:

"We only rent horses until Santa Elena, that's all, and with one of my boys. We no longer rent horses on their own, as there are too many thieves, too many rustlers. Sixty soles for two horses, including the boarding house for tonight and the return trip."

"Will the horses wait for us at Santa Elena?"

"No, the horses and the boy must return immediately'" insisted the old lady.

Once the trip was arranged and after drinking some

simple soup which was almost a stew and tasted delicious, they decided to sleep on mats covered with cow hides on the dirty living room floor. They removed their hats and shoes. Roberto took two towels from his travel bag and folded them to make pillows.

Two more people lived in the simple house: Juano and Balthazar, the old lady's grandsons, who were eighteen and twenty respectively. Juano was to accompany them the next day.

"The old man is resourceful", mused Roberto as he tried to get comfortable on the hard bed. "Where did he get that name from that broke the old lady's suspicion?" He would later discover that Don Fernando had invented the name 'Cornelio' and that 'Alegria' was the surname of the former proprietors of the Marcabal Ranch. The old man knew this because he had spent several weeks there in his youth.

When they awoke at dawn, the horses were already saddled and bridled. Juano – in a hat, poncho and with his saddlebag full of food – was waiting for them.

It had been many years since they were on horseback, but they discovered it was like riding a bicycle: once you learned how to ride, you never forgot. As it was, the entire route was uphill so they could only ride slowly.

The third day of the trip proved the most spectacular for Don Fernando. In some places they followed old Inca trails that were still well-preserved. The paths were extremely narrow and vertiginous at times, and they had to cross the precipices one at a time. Now and then, on turning into a particularly tight bend, the horses' heads seemed to hang over a void, giving an eyrie-like sensation of being suspended in thin air and a real fear of falling off the precipice. Hundreds of metres below, small houses with smoke seeping through their thatched roves could be seen – the locals seldom bothered with chimneys. The men stopped at various times to rest and to share the food from Juano's saddlebag: roasted corn with pork crackling and some apples, washed down with stream water.

On this leg of the journey they ran into no other travellers. The rain didn't slow them down, mostly due to the fact that the boy knew his job and the terrain well, each bend, brook and narrow mountain pass that they travelled through. Juano had said that they would arrive by nightfall, but it was already nearly five o'clock and the sun threatened to disappear within the hour. They picked up pace as it was dangerous to be out after dark. "We've been travelling for almost three days", thought Roberto: "This mountain range is so circuitous. If you draw a straight line to Trujillo, it would be less than one hundred and thirty miles away. An aeroplane could fly this in twenty-five minutes."

Once again, they ran into problems, this time in Santa Elena where they had to leave the horses. "A town of forty inhabitants and eighty dogs" commented Don Fernando jokingly, as the pack of hounds welcomed them by snapping at their animals' hooves. It was already night time and 'Juano' took them to see Don Santos, the owner of the best supplied shop in town. Nobody wanted to rent them horses for the next leg of the journey and Don Fernando enquired discretely as he knew that they were in a danger zone. He felt that "in a town with the hammer and sickle painted on every wall, it was better to behave carefully", particularly among so many strangers that had gathered, attracted by the barking of the dogs.

They made many inquiries about buying rather then renting horses, but it seemed no one wanted to sell their horses either. Finally the only thing that convinced these children of the revolution was the old argument of money. Someone asked three hundred and fifty soles for each animal, nearly three times the going rate. Following the slight nod of his uncle's head, Roberto accepted the price, but under the condition that they could select the animals themselves. This was agreed and that night they slept in hammocks, while keeping a constant eye open.

"Lie down diagonally, like this; so that the surface becomes tight and flat like a bed," Don Fernando advised when he noticed Roberto was having trouble with this new form of bedding.

The sun was already high above their heads when they began the upward path to Marcabal. They had wasted a lot of time with the dishonest Don Santos who knew that nobody would guide them at any price and tried to hide his best horses from them. In the end, they paid eight hundred and thirty soles for two horses, which was fair as they had chosen the best of the lot, including those that he'd hidden. Naturally, Don Fernando was financing the expedition as Roberto would never be able to face the expenses. However, Juano did not charge them a single penny to draw them a rough but serviceable map of how to get to Marcabal.

Lunch was a tin of fish with some bread and lemonade. Their resting place was the ruins of what was once an Inca *tambo*, a lodge for travellers in that Empire, where they could spread their ponchos and have a siesta, allowing the horses and their aching behinds a rest.

They had been riding for hours and the ascent seemed never-ending; the constant fear that they would be captured and detained at any moment by the rebels made the journey no easier. Although neither of them said it, everything seemed to indicate that Marcabal was the headquarters of the Shining Path's north-west brigades; they were now entering the lion's den.

From Juano's useful map, they could calculate that they were only one or two hours away from the ranch. They had seen only one shepherd along the way, who pretended not to speak Spanish and would not give them any directions, he simply shrugged.

MARCABAL

Two men and a couple of exhausted horses made their appearance on the outskirts of the hamlet, where a few houses of adobe and thatch lay clustered together. They had climbed to around ten thousand feet above sea level. Worn out and covered in sweat, they approached the country house that stood on the high part of a promontory where extensive arable land and terraces seemed to have been abandoned. Stretching before them, as far as their eyes could see were magnificent mountains, lush with vegetation washed up from the Amazon basin beyond.

A sign announced the 'Agrarian Production Co-operative of Marcabal Grande'; it looked more like an epitaph on the dirty white-brownish façade, stained from the mud that had seeped down through the broken roof tiles. It was around six thirty in the evening and the sun had still not gone down completely. Not a soul appeared on the deserted street but in the nearby houses faces seemed to peep out from behind doorways and windows.

They reached the country house's main gate and were surprised that nobody came out to meet them. The thought of an ambush crossed their minds. Roberto leapt down from his horse and helped the old man dismount. "Tough old man", he thought, "to have made it all the way here."

The silence was sporadically interrupted by the whistle of the wind that mercilessly whipped this mountaintop, giving the impression that even the dogs didn't dare to bark. They heard a faint drumming, as if someone in the house was using an old typewriter. "Good evening", Roberto called, almost screaming, as he gingerly passed the threshold of the door that stood ajar. Nobody answered but the drumming stopped abruptly. Suddenly, a female voice, with the tone and ring to it of an older person from another era, called out:

"Who is it?"

"Outsiders searching for information and lodging," replied Roberto.

A figure from another epoch that resembled a ghostly apparition slowly approached them. Before them was an old lady of medium height with hair as white as snow and the delicate features of her pink face woven with fine wrinkles. She was dressed in black and her appearance, although sad, was not uncared for. "She must be seventy-six years old and was probably very beautiful when she was young," thought Roberto.

"How may I help you gentlemen?" she asked in a pleasant and polite voice.

They did not know how to reply. They were confused as both of them had expected something else, another type of reception. What they had envisioned was being suddenly detained and handcuffed, perhaps pointed at with machine guns and dragged before bearded characters in combat uniforms. The lady noticed their bewilderment and added:

"My name is Rosalinda Alegria and I am in charge of this house."

Her eyes were fixed on Don Fernando and this seemed to disturb him. She asked again:

"Is there something I can do for you?"

"Yes, ma'am", said Roberto at last, "my uncle and I need board and lodging for a few days. We would like to explore the possibility of transporting cattle from Marañón to 'El Pallar'. We will only stay a few days, maybe two or three..."

The conversation was suddenly interrupted by the

sounds of a galloping horse and the arrival of a horseman who reined in abruptly, causing the horse to spin around in front of the gate. The animal was soaked in sweat and breathing rapidly, its nostrils dilated and its exhausted body steaming, a sign that it had been galloping almost until it dropped. The horseman dismounted and rushed up to them, nearly pushing them further inside. Taking off his hat he exclaimed:

"Dad, Uncle. What has happened? Is my mother all right?"

Recovering from the shock and taking a second to recognise him, Roberto answered:

"Yes son, she is all right, we all are."

"So then, what is this madness? What are you doing here?" inquired the young Juan Carlos nervously.

Roberto observed that the lady, upon seeing that it was his son, withdrew softly, almost floating down the hallway. He waited for an instant and explained to his son that he needed to talk to him urgently, man to man; and looking at the old man, as if apologising, added: "but your uncle insisted on coming".

Juan Carlos took them both by the arm and led them to the huge dark living room, sparsely furnished with a few crude benches. Without doubt, the place had seen better days and the benches, from their rudimentary look, could not possibly have been the original furniture of the house. Juan Carlos's appearance surprised Roberto. He looked stronger, sported a beard, long hair, and moved around as if very familiar with the mansion.

As soon as they sat down, Roberto looked around to make sure that they were alone and asked in a hushed voice:

"How did you know that we were coming?"

"One of our men who arrived at noon informed me about your trip, giving me your names as suspicious intruders. He travelled with you on the truck from Huamachuco and saw you get off at 'El Pallar'. He then continued on to Sartín, and took a shorter route to a nearby spot. He spent the night here and made his way down to our base this morning."

Roberto and his uncle looked at each other in surprise. Which one would he be? Was he the one who sat apart? Did he hear the dialogue between the quota collectors and Don Fernando? *"If he heard that"*, they thought, *"We're in trouble."* But perhaps he had believed their story, just like the quota collectors. It would be better to tell Juan Carlos right away.

"Before we tell you why we have come", said Roberto, "I think you should know about something that happened on the way here that could put us all in serious danger. When those young men" – he didn't want to say 'rebels' – "who charge the quota went through uncle's papers, the one who inspected his ID looked at him intently and asked him if he was a Del Mar from the coach factory?" My uncle replied that he wished he was, but unfortunately he was related to the poor side of the Del Mar family, the ones that have to travel by truck. The guy gave him his ID back with a smile and left."

Juan Carlos thought it over. "Damn. Yes, it could be dangerous. But I don't remember telling anyone at camp that we are related."

Roberto hesitated about saying more as he was not completely sure that they were alone, and was afraid that someone might hear them.

"Where are the others? Where is the camp? Why do you move around as though you own this place?" asked Roberto.

The young man looked at his father and then his great-uncle inquisitively for a long time. *"What is behind all this?"* he wondered. No, he couldn't doubt his own father, or his old uncle. Surely, the son-of-a-bitch military wouldn't have forced them, blackmailed them maybe, to come here just to locate the operational headquarters. Maybe the two were wired with ultra-sensitive radios, and once the military had the information that they were after, they would rescue them and bomb the base.

To the astonishment of his elder relatives, Juan Carlos disconnected the walkie-talkie that they use sometimes, walked away and returned with a pencil and a piece of paper on which he had written: "Do you give me your word of honour that nobody has made you come here? Only reply in writing." He handed them the paper and pencil.

"Of course nobody has" wrote Roberto and added: "I swear it by Carla. Are you sure that we can talk here?"

"Sure," he affirmed without using the pen or paper, "except for the old lady who is in her room and two lookouts on the top of the house, there are only two peasant families in the surrounding area".

Now Roberto felt relieved and his son, to reassure his relatives, began to answer their questions.

"The camp is in Collona, almost half a day by horse from here. This place is only a lookout post and the watchmen knew about your arrival. I told them a few hours ago by walkie-talkie, and said that you were important people to the cause; that is why they didn't shoot or intercept you. The old lady is the last survivor of the family that owned these lands and refused to leave the house when her relatives and some of the workers fled. She is a strange and interesting woman who reads a lot and sympathises with our cause but most people think she is half mad. The house and the surroundings are abandoned; we hardly ever use them."

Don Fernando was suffering from an internal struggle; he was not sure if he should share it with the others or not. After a while he decided that he should:

"I know that lady, although I have not seen her for nearly sixty years. I don't know if she has recognised me, and if she has, I don't know if she knows who I am today."

Roberto thought to himself "Oh God. Uncle's presence has complicated everything. Now anything may happen".

169

"She was very pretty and we used to talk a lot; I think that she fell in love with me, felt compassion for me or something like that. I think that I was afraid to fall in love and anyway she was unattainable for me as the social gap was huge. Frankly, I thought that she had died long ago as I never heard of her again."

At that moment, Rosalinda was reading in her untidy room surrounded by old books. She tried to read the latest manifesto of President Gonzalo, the Shining Path's leader, but she found her mind wandering and she seemed to be elsewhere. A faint smile adorned her wrinkled face.

Meanwhile, Comrade Raul, Juan Carlos's boss, had found out about the visitors and deduced – by his surname, approximate age, and the description that he had given – that the old man must be the well-known industrialist. He also knew that Juan Carlos had disappeared under the pretext that he was going to check up on the lookout points. And although he did not have a clear idea of what they had planned and why they had come from so far, he could imagine that they had come for the boy which naturally was to the detriment of the movement. He was aware that Juan Carlos was an upright militant, but his defection, especially with his knowledge of the organisation, would be extremely dangerous for them, particularly now after President Gonzalo's capture that they were without a leader.

Due to one of those strange twists of destiny, 'Comrade Raul' happened to be Alejandro Morey, the son of a brilliant and well known Peruvian Naval Officer: Admiral Augusto Morey, in charge of antiterrorism. Admiral Morey one day appeared on a nationwide television programme to be interviewed about his rebel son. At the beginning he appeared calm and composed but, overwhelmed by the circumstances, the difficulty of the questions and the fact that it was his only child, he started to become ill at easy and dramatically challenged his son through a now well-known appeal:

"My dearest son, you know me well as an honest and down to earth warrior. You know that I have sworn loyalty to our country to the very end, and as such I have the duty and moral obligation to destroy the infamous movement you embrace. So, here and now I beg you to surrender and give up your arms. In the event that you do not agree with this sincere appeal that I am making on behalf of your devastated mother and myself, there is nothing else to discuss but to advise you that if one day, God forbid, we meet head-on, you need to shoot me first."

The rebel now found himself with the heavy responsibility of having to eliminate his own comrade; the movement could not take any more risks. At the same time he thought, "We will try to capture the old man alive, as we need a large number of important prisoners to exchange for our leader." He considered that four men equipped with automatic weapons, as well as the watchmen, would be more than enough to do the job, assuming that neither the old man nor the father would be armed and that Juan Carlos was only carrying his Magnum 44. Not wanting to waste any time, they departed in a hurry around five in the evening, planning to arrive at the house at ten or ten thirty that night.

"We have come to beg you to come home with us", explained Roberto calmly, trying to sound persuasive. "It is not worth dying for a lost cause."

Juan Carlos stood up suddenly, and stared at his elders in amazement. He was livid and his eyes bulged from their sockets. Trying not to shout, he declared:

"What? You have come for that? You have risked so much to come here to waste your time? No, I am not going anywhere. No sir. I will stay here until our cause triumphs. This is a matter of victory or death; I thought that you understood that, father."

"That is right, son, I thought that I understood it and if I were your age, you can be sure that I would also be here. However, recent events have occurred that seriously question the purpose of our revolution."

"What are you talking about? Do you mean the capture of President Gonzalo? *Mierda!* Shit. They will pay a high price for whatever they do to him. His capture was only a temporary mishap anyway - our battle continues with or without him, until the final victory. Our movement is growing each day and we are still winning the war."

"That is what clandestine left-wing papers and magazines say."

"What? And you, who do you believe now? the lies of the reactionary press?"

Don Fernando cleared his throat and interrupted:

"Your father is right, son, and I am sure that you are also right by saying that you don't believe what the media of the right publishes. We all agree that not everything that is written in the press can be taken seriously. Allow me to quote George Bernard Shaw, who said that "Reading made Don Quixote a gentleman, but believing what he read made him mad". Therefore, in order to hold a serious conversation like intelligent people, let us analyse the actual facts, the proven realities of the situation, not what is irresponsibly published. We won't analyse Guzman's capture either if you wish".

"Uncle, with all the due respect that I have for you, allow me to doubt your reasoning. You don't have the problems that the poor have, you don't suffer what they suffer; therefore, your bourgeois mentality and self-interested reasoning leads you to different conclusions, out of your ignorance of the basic premises. Many of you believe that you 'think', when all you are doing is 'reordering' your prejudices."

"You must have been told, JC, that I have not always been rich and that the poverty that I knew when young was far more dramatic and sad than the one you know." Don

172

Fernando addressed the young man using his family nickname. "You are correct in the first part of what you say. Many of us think or believe that we 'think'; that is precisely why I suggest that we analyse the raw facts leaving aside prejudices, stereotypes or clichés as a waste of time.

"Today's world is different from yesterday's world and from the one that you left when you decided to take up arms. Tomorrow's world will be even more different. You know what I am referring to: the dynamics of history, events such as the end of the Cold War, a consequence of the fall of the Soviet Union and other socialist countries; events that our country can't be isolated from. Because of the technological revolution in media, the world is now a smaller, more predictable, but more dangerous place. These events and the ones that are being generated are going to change," affirmed the octogenarian, "and are constantly changing the face of the earth for better or worse, whether we want it or not."

"Do you think that it is intelligent to swim against the current by following an ideology that – as admirable and romantic as it is – has not led to anything better than the misery and destruction of so many people's hopes and to their economic ruin? Do you think that well-meaning people would ignore Gorbachev's confessions to the world in the sense that: "For a long time we thought that we were right about everything, but reality cruelly showed us how wrong we were."

"Sorry to interrupt you, uncle, but the fact that I took up arms and went underground did not isolate me from what happens in the world. We are completely informed, through short wave radios, of what is happening in the world and what traitors, like the son-of-a-bitch that you mention, comment. This is a battle between the oppressed majority and a parasitic, exploiting minority, between the poor and the rich of the world. Therefore, whether the Cold War ends or not, whether there is a strain between the East and the West, our battle will continue while this state of affairs persists."

"You are right again," affirmed the old man, "the tension is not between the East and the West now; the tension is between the South and the North, the poor South against the rich North. And this state of affairs will continue, I agree with you, but within another form, and it must thus be fought with other weapons. We humans are as imperfect as the systems we use or invent. Nobody is right forever. And again, what is good today will not necessarily be so tomorrow, we have to understand this dynamic."

"I am not an ultra conservative old man who is saying that the past was better and that we should conserve the present by isolating ourselves from changes," added Don Fernando, "not at all. I am telling you the opposite; everything changes and will continue to do so. My suggestion is to identify those changes, those winds; let's see where they are headed and adapt to them, take advantage of them, and not fight against them. We should be humble as we are too small and insignificant in number to try to change the course of history; the world is now just one entity."

Juan Carlos was almost shouting now: "Of course, so we should thus abandon our noble cause, abandon the battle and let the powerful abuse the weak. No uncle that is for cowards, life is not worth living that way. Don't ask me to accept abuse, corruption and this indifference forever," replied the rebel.

"On the contrary, we should never stop fighting", affirmed Don Fernando in a very low voice. "The difference is how we fight, where, and against whom. And most importantly, how are we going to win? Because we have to win, isn't that true? Because wars are like football, winning is not the most important thing. It is the *only* important thing. To fight for the sake of fighting is to waste one's time and, sometimes, one's life for nothing" He paused to give JC time to assimilate the sense of this last part of his argument, and then continued "I fight when I am convinced that I will win; if not, I don't do it, why should I?"

"Modern wars", continued the old man, "are no longer fought on battlefields. Now they are fought in world markets: by penetrating them, winning them to create jobs, and thus creating wealth that benefits everybody. The weapons that are used are also different: intelligence, knowledge and audacity are now necessary"

"That sacred anger that we have, that energy that moves mountains, must be channelled so that we can get out of this underdevelopment alone, with nobody else's help, since nobody is going to help us anyway. This is a task for the brave, for the real machos. That is where we must take the gamble, by not giving quarter to poverty. The abuse, corruption and opportunism that worry you – as it worries all other well-meaning men – must be banished. However, the system that you want to implement won't get rid of these problems. I have seen that sort of corruption, abuse, prostitution and indifference dominate socialist countries; they were never able to banish them. Instead, they seemed to flourish. Anyway, we are not here to discuss these facts, but to reason more deeply", he added.

"After Poland, Hungary and the rest of the eastern European countries liberated themselves from the communist yoke; East Germany began to stagger and was only able to hold on because of their leader Erich Honecker's iron fist and pathological will. It was then that Gorbachev told him something that convinced him to let go the reins of power: "History never forgives those who arrive late". Now I tell you," said Don Fernando firmly, "life doesn't forgive those who realise too late, those who stubbornly and irrationally continue along the wrong path."

"Oh God," thought Roberto, "now I understand why the old man was so sure he could convince Juan Carlos."

Don Fernando's arguments had produced huge confusion in Juan Carlos's mind; he remained silent for a while with his mind in turmoil, because on top of the powerful reasons given, he now had to consider that it wasn't just his own life in danger but those of his father and uncle too. Should his father's political stand be even in a small way in agreement with his, and the uncle not present, he thought he might be able to explain his absence to comrade Raul and try to get away with it; but what made that impossible, was his father's strong opposition to the warfare. And as if these problems were not enough, there was his uncle's great appeal as a negotiating chip. This last consideration was of the greatness weight to Raul.

It was already late; they had not eaten and were starving. The dying light of a kerosene oil lamp burning on the table scared away the shadows of the huge living room, where they had been talking, for nearly two hours

"What do you think, father?" asked the young man after a while.

"I agree with your uncle, son. I think that there is no worse blind man than the one who doesn't want to see. Our country does not need more destruction. It needs peace, tranquillity and progress. I think that our battle should be in another area and that, although our problems are immense, we must overcome them. But that will only be possible if we all pull the rope in the same direction. Only in that way will we vindicate our anonymous heroes, such as our adored Carla who, in her own way, died for a better Peru."

The mention of his sister upset Juan Carlos and he lent forward with his elbows on his knees, and began to wring his hands slowly as he stared at the dirty wooden floor; without shifting position, he now reclined his chin on one hand and remained in this position for a long time. His eyes were facing the large windows of the house but seeing nothing, he closed them and went into deep thought.

It must have been around ten o'clock at night; a fierce flash-storm started outside with much thunder and lightning. Rosalinda still hadn't gone to bed; her small reading spectacles on the tip of her nose, she continued to read under the weak light of a lamp. In reality, she only read bits and pieces, as she could not concentrate. Not because of the storm that drummed furiously against the tiles on the roof and the panes of her window... There was something on her mind that changed the expression on her face, as if a ray of light had finally penetrated the shadows of a dark room that had been closed for years.

"Fernando, it is you, it can be no other... you have finally come. I have waited so long."

In her youth she met, one can't say many, but yes several suitors; she liked some of them and thought herself in love. But her father – an old-fashioned and dominant man – found none of them suitable. A candidate would have to be white, educated and from a good family; preferably from Trujillo. Also, she was not to marry any of her cousins, even though her family had done so for generations precisely because of the lack of acceptable suitors. Some men appeared who seemed to satisfy all the necessary requirements. But then her father would comment sternly "but he is not from Trujillo...", and when he was from Trujillo he would say, "He can't come from a good family, otherwise he would not be around here". He only took her to Trujillo on two or three occasions and for a very short period of time. As a consequence, Rosalinda, because of her education and obedience, remained trapped at home.

When her father died, Rosalinda had grown old and she no longer seemed to be interested in men; she became devoted to helping her widowed mother and managed the *hacienda*, along with her bachelor brother. The rest of the six siblings had abandoned their home one by one to marry and live in Huamachuco or Trujillo.

Then Velasco's socialist revolution had come, with his agrarian reform that took everything away from them: their land, their harvests, their livestock and their home. Thanks to the kindness of some workers who were fond of them and were not afraid to show it, they were still allowed to use part of the house. Her mother had died much later and eventually so did her brother, when the hordes of President Gonzalo were devastating what even the agrarian reform had not been able to destroy with its idleness and incompetence.

Rosalinda rose and headed towards the main dormitory, which once belonged to her parents. She set up the camp beds for the watchmen to sleep on, although they sometimes threw the mattresses on the floor to make love.

Making their way to Marcabal, the combatants under Raul's command continued relentlessly to push their exhausted horses on and advanced painfully in the rain. Raul looked at his watch and saw that it was 10:25 at night, the time by which they should have already been surrounding the house.

DECISIONS

"In the last minute of his life, crossed by a hellish fire power that lasted a thousandth of a second, only God knows if he thought of his parents, his friend, or in the revolution's success."

After hours of anguished meditation, Juan Carlos had reached the conclusion that his older relatives might be right but he remained undecided and wondered: It might be true what they say, but if so then what did the heroes of the Spanish Civil War die for? And the heroes in Vietnam? And Che Guevara? It was true, China was the only communist country that could be called successful; but its success had been attained through capitalism and not through communism. And if this was no longer a war fought for a noble cause, then was it for vengeance?

Roberto and his son, Comrade Rodrigo – as he was known in the area- were standing with their arms crossed, father and son both lost in their own dilemmas. They stood contemplating the unleashed forces of nature through the large windows. "Storms pass in a moment, they do not last forever", thought the father. "And that is how it should be with the storm of disasters that our country has suffered for so long. Dear God, help me to get my son out of all this. Please don't allow him to make a useless sacrifice. Take me and leave him to fight for his people in a more civilised way. I give you my life for his," he implored.

Juan Carlos was wondering how he would inform his

superiors if he decided to leave the movement, and what the implications would be. He felt a deep grief even contemplating the idea. When he had thought about it in the past, because at times, he had to admit, he really had thought about deserting, what hurt him most was the prospect of abandoning his dreams of a better Peru; he had idealised the future.

It was these dreams that had kept him in the struggle. That was why he told himself that his cause was a noble one, because he was not fighting for himself but for his countrymen. But the anger and desire for vengeance that he had initially felt had gradually disappeared; his spirit was too noble to harbour such lowly desires. "Such a laborious and noble country, forced to its knees by adversity. No, damn it, it can't be." he thought.

Don Fernando, for once in his life, didn't really know what to do; he felt that the first part of the plan, of convincing his nephew, had been almost attained, it was just a matter of time. Now he had to think about the next stage: to escape as soon as possible. While he gave Juan Carlos time to reach his own decision, he paced with slow steps along a corridor and thought of Rosalinda all those years ago. "I must have been in love, but I am sure that I never told her because I was afraid to. When I left, my feelings faded due to distance and time. Should I tell her now? Is it worth it? Maybe it will give her some consolation and happiness to know this at the end of her life, but what about the danger? Won't it be dangerous for everyone if she knows who I am?"

It was about ten thirty; there seemed to be no end to the storm and Rosalinda was still awake. She had seen that the watchmen had changed; a young man and woman went up the stairs tugging at each other and laughing while the two they had gone to replace came downstairs, ate their frugal meal and retired to their quarters. The old lady sang in a low voice and opened her trunk, taking out her best dress; it was a long blue velvet low-cut dress, with a tight waist and a full skirt. It must have been very elegant when it was new; sixty or so years ago, when it had not been so stained or discoloured. Incredibly, it still fit her, although she looked like a character out of an old novel. She arranged her hair in an unusual way with a parting on one side which caused her curls to cascade chaotically over her face. She then applied heavy white makeup, painted her lips and donned a blue wide-brim hat; although her spirit was happy and festive, she looked sad and a little grotesque.

Many times in the past Raul and Rodrigo had analysed and discussed the Peruvian situation with passion. "High Society" they call it - a bloody stupidity. As far as I know everyone in this country came to it penniless, empty handed, with one hand covering their genitals and the other one covering their backside." It was comrade Raul speaking, and he continued: "Every one came to make their fortunes here. No one brought a cent; the only families that ever came with their fortunes to invest were the Gildemeisters from Germany and the Swaynes, no one else. The rest have made their wealth and their so called "pedigree" here, mostly abusing and taking advantage of the corrupt judiciary system."

They even had some philosophical discussions - although neither of them were particularly strong in this discipline - as they were both impulsive young men with very strong convictions; psychologists would call them 'emotionally driven' people. Through these discussions they had come to like each other in a fraternal way, or maybe it was because they both came from a similar background and felt different from the rest. All this was weighing a great deal on Rodrigo's mind, delaying his conclusion.

At last, Juan Carlos had already made his decision: he would desert and leave immediately with his elder relatives as it would be extremely dangerous to wait any longer. He knew there were three available horses outside which should be rested by now. They would leave in a few minutes; after the horses were saddled up he felt he should write a letter to his superiors explaining his motives. "Although no deserter is left alive," he thought, "I will not betray them."

Comrade Raul definitely did not believe this and he was furious. The storm and the mud had delayed their ascent up the mountain and made it seem never-ending. The tired horses kept slipping on the sodden ground and they still had not reached the peak where the country house stood. "Damn it Rodrigo! You fucking traitor, how did you do this to us?" "After I have the old man in my power I will disembowel you with my own hands, you bastard." He checked his watch and saw that it was 10:58. Rounding a bend and straining to see through the rain, they could make out the lights of the old house, about half a mile away. They were surprised that the lights were still on; but they saw it as a good omen, a sign that their quarry were still there. "In ten or fifteen minutes we will have the house surrounded," figured Raul: "But first we must make contact with the watchmen."

While Juan Carlos tried to write his letter, Roberto stretched out on a bench and tried to sleep. The chimes from the antique grandfather clock struck eleven times and Don Fernando, seated in the freezing cold, continued to wrestle with his thoughts: "She must have suffered so much. It would do her good to chat and remember her youth. What a pity that she will never know that I remembered her and that I loved her in my own way." He got up slowly and walked back and forth in a pensive manner. By chance, or by one of those strange coincidences in life, he had reached the lady's room at the same moment that she opened the door, and, holding a lamp above her head, signalled for him to enter. A chill ran down his spine and paralysed the old man momentarily.

"Come in, Fernando. How have you been? Sit down, I was waiting for you."

Without regaining his composure, he approached her trembling and sat on a chair beside the bed where she was sitting. With a nervous smile he said:

"I did not think that you would recognise me. How are you? So many years have gone by."

"Far too many, Fernando" She seemed to enjoy pronouncing his name. "I always asked about you, but nobody gave me any information. Some told me that you were very rich and later on I heard that you had died. I was so sad."

The old man made no comment. He was completely absorbed in the moment; he thought of what life does to people - the merciless way in which it sometimes treated them and the deep deformities that it inflicted upon their appearance. Wanting to offer her some happiness he said:

"You used to be very beautiful, Rosalinda. I had never seen beauty and grace such as yours. Your social standing was so high for me that, out of fear that you would be offended or make fun of me, I never told you that I liked you and that I was in love with you."

Don Fernando felt the lady's bony hand on his own, squeezing it lightly. He did not know what to do; now that he had transmitted his message he thought that he should withdraw. He was about to get up when he felt her hand hold him back.

"I also fell in love with you and loved you very much, Fernando. I often dreamed of you to the point that I idealised you. When I saw you this afternoon, although you are, of course, older and somewhat different, I recognised your eyes. How could I forget them? As always, they were so serene."

He tried to withdraw but felt her tug again.

"Don't be afraid, I know that you are married. I got my hopes up high, but like all good and bad things in life, I have learned how to live with, and without them".

"Rosalinda, I didn't know how to tell you without offending you. It has been an immense pleasure to see you again. I did not expect it; I had no idea where you now were; you know, it has been nearly sixty years since I last saw you. I thank God that he gave me this surprise and satisfaction, but I must leave; my relatives and I will be away at any minute."

The lady remained pensive and sad and said:

"Rodrigo is a good kid. He is so different from the rest. They think that I support them but I hate them. They have tormented my life and I have to pretend that I am on their side. How can they believe all this trash they read? The more I read it the more convinced I am that they are completely wrong. But, why contradict them? One day I will really go crazy and they will get to know the real me, they will start to pay for their abuses. They don't even respect the elderly. They are evil; except for a few exceptions they are cruel... They say that they fight for peace and justice. But we all want peace to rule. Do you know what peace is? She is the daughter of justice, and if there is no mother there is no daughter. Oh, Fernando. I think that I also have to thank God for allowing me to see you again. If someone had asked me for my last wish before dying, you know what it would have been? To see you again"

Comrade Raul and his men were already surrounding the house. But in spite of trying continuously, they had not been able to establish contact with the watchmen through the walkie-talkies. Raul cursed the storm and looked at his watch: it was 11:12. The rain continued to pour down and the dogs barked at ear-splitting levels, as if they had seen the devil. He and his men were restless and worried that the watchmen would mistake them as enemies and open fire.

Meanwhile in the look-out post, a walkie-talkie rattled on the ground with messages that were drowned out by the storm; neither 'Tatiana' nor 'Julian', the youngsters' chosen combat names, heard it. They were fast asleep, drunk and exhausted from their lovemaking.

In spite of the distant explosions of thunder, the barking dogs had already alerted Juan Carlos that something was happening outside. He woke his father and whispered instructions in his ear. They got some ropes and tiptoed barefoot to the room where the rebels who had already ended their shift lay sleeping; they woke to find their own machine guns pointing at them. Juan Carlos tied their hands and feet and gagged them. They left them covered with blankets and bolted the door from the outside.

When Juan Carlos and Roberto turned around, they met their uncle and the old lady in the hallway, had come to see what was happening on hearing the commotion outside. Juan Carlos hesitated for a moment and then advanced towards the lady in order to tie her up as well. Don Fernando, although he did not know what had just happened, guessed his intentions and stood in front of her saying: "Wait a moment, she is one of us." A few seconds of silence passed as a confused Juan Carlos looked into the eyes of the old, elegant marionette, and Don Fernando intervened again:

"Juan Carlos, trust me, I know her well".

The young man followed his old uncle's advice and left the old woman alone. He now told them, cupping his hands in front of his mouth to neutralise the noises of the storm and the distressing barks of the dogs that they were under imminent attack.

Outside, the dogs continued to howl furiously, but Raul and his people had decided not to attack yet in order to avoid a shoot-out with their own watchmen inside. It would be extremely difficult to coordinate actions, and they knew that any ensuing crossfire would put them in danger. They were nervous and impatient and when they saw the lights go out in the house, Raul felt they had no choice but to go ahead with the attack; he was sure that those inside had already noticed their presence.

A heavier sort of sadness and disillusion overwhelmed Juan Carlos when he saw Raul giving instructions outside. He would have preferred that anybody else but Raul had come for him. In the back of his mind he kept having this sort of wishful thinking. "Unbelievable the strange twists and turns that life takes, now destiny has changed the characters of this story and instead of Raul's father it is now me who should say: You will need to shoot me first, Raul," thought Juan Carlos.

Juan Carlos remembered his walkie-talkie and went to fetch it. When he switched it on he picked up Raul's unsuccessful attempts to establish contact with the watchmen. He briefly thought of communicating with Raul to try to start a dialogue but decided that it was too late.

Raul quickly evaluated the situation; although the element of surprise was no longer on their side, they still had the advantage of greater numbers. He fired his gun into the air to call the watchmen's attention but to no avail. He then fired a burst from his machine gun and only then did the drunkards wake up with a jolt. Looking around in a daze, they headed to where the shots seemed to originate. At that moment Tatiana and Julian made contact with the attackers via walkie-talkie; they were told to go down into the house and capture Comrade Rodrigo and those with him, dead or alive. Juan Carlos couldn't believe his ears when he heard the order given by his old friend on his walkie-talkie.

Rosalinda knew where the weapons were kept and she got hold of two more machine guns. All of them were now armed and sheltering behind a barricade of tables and upturned furniture. They waited for an attack at any moment and from any direction. Inside the house, the atmosphere was very dark and tense; they could just see what was happening outside; Raul's group were huddling under the cornice of the granary's roof, near the kitchen, soaking wet and heavily armed.

The watchmen carefully began to descend the old stairs

that led to the living room; a rotten step creaked at the weight of one of the terrorists, alerting Rosalinda that they were closing in. She slowly got up, took position and aimed, while Carlos agonised, bit his lips. A worn boot appeared on the first visible step, then another. They were only ten feet away and the old lady, with all the calmness in the world, waited until their entire bodies appeared before giving them a fierce and bloody reception. The hammering of the automatic weapon lasted only a second; she had fired in two full sweeps, aiming from one side to another and then back again before the bodies rolled heavily down the last steps. There was no chance that they were alive. But Rosalinda, remembering the rebels' advice, got ready to "double-check". She aimed again and fired another round; causing the corpses to bounce off the bloody wooden floor in front of Juan Carlos, whose expression was one of grief.

"Something has gone wrong and they have had to act", thought Raul, while he commanded his fighters to wait. Seconds passed and when there was still no communication with the watchmen, he imagined the worst and ordered an attack through the kitchen; he left only one man as a reserve, sheltered behind an old overturned cart.

An explosion was heard and they charged, blowing the lock with machine gun bursts, and appeared in the immense living room with their weapons at the ready; in that same instant they were received with an intense, savage wall of bullets. There was no time for anything, no time to assess the situation and certainly no time to start a dialogue. The only dialogue was between the lethal automatic weapons that clattered furiously in a hell of fire, gunpowder and smoke. Mortally wounded, the rebels continued to shoot although they stood no chance. Raul, disfigured and drowning in his own blood, tried to get up but another burst tore his body in half, while Juan Carlos could hardly contain his tears with his AKM still smoking.

Outside, the nervous backup man listened to the sounds of the battle without having the faintest idea who was winning. Anxious and with sweaty hands, he clutched at his weapon and prayed.

Only Don Fernando had been seriously wounded, his left arm hanging like a bloody rag; it had been hit by at least two bullets, which were immediately extracted by Juan Carlos with his mountain knife. "The bone is splintered", he said, worried, while he cleaned the wounds using the first-aid kit that the rebels kept in the house. He sewed up the gashes, applied gauze and bandages and secured Don Fernando's arm to his chest. The possibility of infection was great and they needed professional help urgently.

The attack had been devastating to the old house; rain and freezing wind were now coming through the broken glass of the windows and blowing the filthy curtains around. The mutilated bodies of the terrorists lay in pools of blood and water.

The desperate survivors now prepared to leave; after recharging their weapons they were about to go outside to fetch the horses, but realized that first they had to deal with the man hiding outside behind the cart.

Rosalinda now assumed that her miserable life would not be worth a penny if she stayed in the house. When the terrorists discovered what had happened, they would kill her in the cruellest way imaginable; she knew them too well. Juan Carlos was of the same opinion and planned to take her with them, no matter what.

The spinster, however, had a different plan. She knew that there was only one way to gain precious time and to clear the way, and that was to provoke the sentinel into coming out of his hiding place; otherwise he would remain hidden for God knows how long. So, in her antique clothes and high heels, with a bizarre hat still balanced precariously on her head, she clutched her weapon to her chest and disappeared into the storm, heading towards the terrorist. By the time Juan Carlos and his father noticed what she was up to, they had no alternative but to cover her from where they were standing with their own guns.

When the terrorist saw her approaching, with her weapon at the ready, he leaned out of his hiding place to get a better shooting angle and received a burst of gunfire that caused him to collapse face downwards; mortally wounded and lying in the mud, he stealthily rolled over and aimed his firearm at Rosalinda, who was now only a few steps away. The old lady received the full impact of his fire and after a few macabre dance steps fell heavily into the mud. Juan Carlos raised his weapon once more, aimed, and killed the rebel. Leaping over the puddles he reached the fallen woman and desperately felt the old lady's pulse for signs of life; then he kissed her hand and gently lowered it to the ground.

Juan Carlos and his father carried the old lady and laid her out near the house, under the overhanging eaves of the roof that would protect her from the rain. Don Fernando, who only caught them up with extreme difficulty, respectfully closed her eyes with his free hand, and then he leaned over and gently kissed her peaceful face.

The return home was downhill and dangerous; the rain continued to stream down, soaking them to the skin, and there was almost no visibility. The only way they could get their bearings was when lightning struck and lit up the area for a second. Juan Carlos and his father walked, pulling the horses along and trying not to slide down the treacherous slope. Don Fernando was the only person on horseback; he was tied on to his mount with a rope to prevent him falling off if he fell asleep. The old man and Roberto had not rested in twenty hours, but adrenaline kept them alert.

The storm had finally passed but the quagmire that it had left behind made for a gruelling journey. Their greatest worry was the state of the old man who was in urgent need of a rest; ironically though they needed to keep him awake. Nevertheless the old man, although speaking with great difficulty, kept on talking. Asked by Juan Carlos, who was still shaken by the nightmare they had just left behind, when things had started to go wrong in Peru, the industrialist reflected:

"It happened when our Spanish ancestors arrived. From fanatical religious belief or ignorance, they destroyed the Inca culture instead of assimilating it into their own; the roads the Incas constructed were abandoned, the irrigation systems and terraces that fed their empire were neglected, the great system of distribution of food, clothing and storage of goods was discontinued; in short, when the common economic well-being of the entire population was no longer a priority."

"And how can this be changed?" questioned Juan Carlos trying to keep the old man's thoughts away from the pain that was searing through his arm.

"First, by enforcing the rule of law and then by strengthening the natural advantages that we have, like tourism, it would be much better if people came to spend money that is distributed more widely, reaching everyone and keeping those who would otherwise have emigrated where they are."

The old man couldn't sleep, nor did he wish to. Roberto was now very worried about him, but the old man told him not to worry, that we were born to die.

"I shouldn't speak badly of the Spaniards because, like it or not, the majority of the blood that runs through my veins is Iberian. But that doesn't prevent me from detaching myself from that fact in order to judge them. They, along with the Portuguese, only wanted to get rich, neglecting to impose any rule of law. Do you know why? Because no one can give what they do not have; how could they impose a principle that they hardly knew? Don't forget that for the rest of Europeans until quite recently, Europe ended at the Pyrenees"

Babbling he added: "They didn't do what the English did and come to America with their families…. The

Spaniards left their women behind... As a result while law and order were the basis for English colonies to develop.... and investment in their new land, as they had nobody to send money to... The end result was that the former Iberian colonies of South America are now all Third World countries." However, all this does not justify any of the atrocities committed by the British in their colonies," concluded the exhausted old man.

The effort of conversation demanded too much from the old man and he now fell silent, inclined his head and slowly leaned to one side. Juan Carlos felt the horse become frightened and was able to calm it down. He and his father untied Don Fernando and transferred him to a fresher horse, where he rode supported by Juan Carlos. Roberto also mounted his horse and rode with the reins of the tired animal tied to his saddle. The old man slept or had entered into a coma; it was hard to tell which.

They arrived at Sartín before sunrise just when the horses reached collapsing point. Juan Carlos installed his older relatives in the ruins of the Inca *tambo* about two kilometres outside the town. Juan Carlos explained what he was going to do. He wanted to ride to the nearest town and secure spaces for them on one of the trucks to Huamachuco; he knew that they departed before seven in the morning. It would be a risk to show up with two outsiders who spoke with coastal accents and, even worse, with one of them seriously wounded. They would certainly create suspicion.

By now the headless Shining Path or whatever was left of it in Collona, notified by the horrified peasants who were the first to arrive at the scene of the killing and freed the tied up militants, had taken the decision to go to Marcabal.

After riding the entire night, they went through everything in the old house before setting it on fire. To their surprise, they found an unfinished manuscript typed out by Rosalinda, a kind of long "letter to myself in the future" or a "late revenge" to be found after she died, where she had named the innumerable times some depraved militants had abused her and who they were. To everyone's surprise, one of them was Comrade Raul.

But before Juan Carlos could leave, Roberto took him aside. "I don't think the old man will make it. It's only because he's so tough that he's lasted this far. Look at the blanket he was riding on" and he showed it to him, soaked in blood.

Don Fernando was lying on his side, propped up on an old sack of maize that had been left in the *tambo*. He felt surprisingly calm and detached as what he was sure would be his death approached. Looking at the drawn faces of Roberto and Juan Carlos, who were bending over him, he knew they were trying to disguise their concern. "Don't worry," he said, "it is my time."

He had recovered a bit and in slow motion and uttering with shallow breath, he continued: "I feel our country will be at peace soon….. But will we continue to do what we always do? Living our daily routines and forgetting, as we did before… about the causes that bred terrorism… the monster that has nearly devoured us? …. Aren't we forgetting the hunger and desperation that overwhelm the majority of our fellow countrymen … the conditions that procreated and gave birth to such evil? ….. Can't we adopt a different attitude… and once and for all decide to remove the causes of the problems…… that, whether we like it or not … are still festering?"

Don Fernando looked up at the decayed walls of the Inca *tambo*. The finely chiselled stone ashlars had fallen inwards and ferns and moss grew from the cracks, but one could see that it had once been a building of classical proportions, with the inward-leaning trapezoidal doorway so beloved of the Incas. Beyond, the stone-laid Inca path climbed steeply up towards the mountain-top, hidden by the clouds that were descending all around them.

"So this is how it ends," thought Don Fernando to

himself: "Not under a clear sky, but in the fog." A deep and overwhelming love surged within him for this land whose treasures were scattered and neglected, where the best people were still side-lined by a system that seemed to grind them down without mercy.

The dawn light shining through the clouds around them gave a curious intensity to the faces of his companions. They shone with a luminosity he had never seen before; he had never noticed how Juan Carlos's coffee-coloured eyes were quite so brown, or Roberto's profile so strong, however worn down he had been by the years. He reached out his hand to touch them both.

"Roberto", he said gently: "You should start playing the guitar again." And then he let go.

Juan Carlos lent forward and with a gentle gesture closed the old man's eyes.

Printed in the United Kingdom by
Lightning Source UK Ltd., Milton Keynes
141832UK00001B/15/P